GREAT MOVIES

YOU'VE PROBABLY MISSED

GREAT MOVIES

YOU'VE PROBABLY MISSED

Ardis Sillick and
Michael McCormick

CARROLL & GRAF PUBLISHERS
NEW YORK

GREAT MOVIES YOU'VE PROBABLY MISSED

Carroll & Graf Publishers
An Imprint of Avalon Publishing Group Incorporated
161 William Street, 16th Floor
New York, NY 10038

First Carroll & Graf trade paperback edition (*400 Videos You've Got to Rent*) 1997

Second Carroll & Graf trade paperback edition 2002

Library of Congress Cataloging-in-Publication Data is available.

ISBN: 0-7867-0981-2

Printed in the United States of America
Distributed by Publishers Group West

For Ed, with thanks

Acknowledgments

We'd like to express our sincere appreciation to The Video Warehouse for providing us with easy access to their outstanding video collection, with special thanks to Shannon Jackson, Allan Olney, and Kathy Wunschel for their time and effort.

We'd also like to thank the management and staff of the Cedar Rapids Public Library for their assistance and encouragement, with special thanks to Mary Azeltine and Jerry Hopkins for giving us access to their excellent video collection.

For their suggestions and kindnesses, our thanks to:

Richard and Pat Acton, Bob Cuthbertson, Mark Cuthbertson, Maxene Cuthbertson, Ed and Carol Gorman, Ruth Halterman, Carol Hepner, Scott Hepner, Teresa Hepner, Jerry Hopkins, Ed Jackson, Roy and Joyce Kenagy, Tom Lockwood, Mark Long, Dori McLaughlin, Chuck Mitchell, Barbara Nassif, Rob Nassif, Dick and Judy Neiman, Deb Oline, Merle and Harriet Picht, Allan Sillick, Brian Sillick, Helen Sillick, Kevin Sillick, Becky Stamy, and Jim Tomasik.

And finally, many thanks to those who generously contributed their own lists of favorite overlooked movies for the book:

Chuck Barris, Lawrence Block, Randy Sue Coburn, Tom Disch, David Freeman, John Greenfeld, Charlie Haas, A. E. Hotchner, Joe and Victoria Klein, Greil Marcus, Stephen J. Rivele, Gay Talese, Lucian K. Truscott IV, Kenneth Turan, and Jonathan Yardley.

Contents

Introduction

You've decided to venture beyond the confines of the "Current Releases" shelf at your local video store. You want to see something good, of course. Something you haven't seen before. Something that doesn't star Arnold Schwarzenegger. Maybe something a bit unusual. We've all been there. If you take the time to browse through those rows and rows of videos, how do you know that what you eventually find will be worth seeing? Or do you read your Maltin's video guide from cover to cover, writing down titles to look for next time? The strength of those huge, comprehensive video guides is also their weakness—there are thousands of titles to search through, good, bad, and indifferent, to find something you might want to see. That's what this book is about.

Here you'll find hundreds of recommended movies, old and new, that you've probably missed at the theater and the video store. Overlooked, forgotten, or underappreciated for no good reason, these movies should be seen and enjoyed. This isn't a guide to the obscure and the offbeat, we've tried to include a wide variety of movies, from every genre, all with one thing in common—they offer rich rewards.

There are movies that failed at the box office, not because they were turkeys, but because they were savaged by the critics, or had a confusing title, lukewarm promotion, or in some cases, the movie may have been a little ahead of its time. Movies like William Friedkin's *Sorcerer,* the nail-biter remake of the French action classic *The Wages of Fear.* Critics trashed it in comparison with the original, and the title suggests something closer to Friedkin's hit *The Exorcist* than a jungle adventure, and audiences stayed away. But time has been good to it and it stands on its own as pulse-pounding entertainment. Or

there's Francis Ford Coppola's 1974 masterpiece, *The Conversation,* one of the great films of the 1970s starring Gene Hackman, that got lost between Parts I and II of his monumental *Godfather* saga.

Then there are the independent and foreign films that have such limited distribution that it requires vigilance and a will to find them at movie theaters or as they're shown sporadically on cable. Movies like *Thousand Pieces of Gold,* or the charming *Ruby in Paradise* with Ashley Judd, and all of John Sayles's movies.

We haven't separated foreign movies into a separate category because we think they should be listed within genres, like everything else. Foreign films are an untapped resource of entertainment for American audiences. *The Killer* was filmed in Chinese, but it's a magnificent action picture. Or there's *Pathfinder,* a Norwegian film, bristling with adventure. We've indicated if a movie is subtitled or dubbed, but we generally recommend the subtitled versions since dubbing is usually so poorly done.

There are also some wonderful older movies here, some of them classics, that may sound familiar or that you've possibly seen, like *Brief Encounter* or *The Haunting,* or the delightful Alec Guinness comedies from the 1950s like *The Ladykillers,* or *The Lavender Hill Mob.* If you've never had the chance to see them, please do. And if you're aging boomers like we are, you may have seen them thirty years ago, or more. See them again and you'll find the experience even more enriching than you remember.

We strongly recommend that you take a look at movies in genres that you don't think you enjoy. If you don't like the violence of most action movies, try one of the wonderful adventure films that the whole family can enjoy, like *The Crimson Pirate,* or *The Flame and the Arrow.* If you're not a Western fan, and many women think they're not, try *Ride the High Country* or *The Ballad of Little Jo.* And even if you don't have kids in the house, investigate the Family section. There are movies here that everyone will love.

We've only included movies in our recommendations that have at some time been released on video. Not all of them may be available right now; this changes from month to month. There's probably no one store that will carry all of these movies, but most should be available if you check around. If you're lucky, as we are, you have access to a public library with a good video collection.

We all know the joy of the unexpected discovery, and the two of us have taken great pleasure over the years in finding these underappreciated movies and sharing them with friends. We're happy to be able to share them with you.

Action /Adventure

ACROSS 110TH STREET

1972

DIRECTOR: Barry Shear.

SCREENPLAY: Luther Davis, from the novel by Wally Ferris.

CAST: Anthony Quinn, Yaphet Kotto, Anthony Franciosa, Paul Benjamin, Ed Bernard.

Color, R rated, 102m.

Warfare erupts in Harlem when three black men rob the Mafia. Yaphet Kotto is the young, by-the-book lieutenant who's put in charge of the case, and Quinn is a coarse, aging detective who's willing to cut corners to get the job done. Their battle of wills over who'll call the shots reflects the racial hostility in their community. This is brutal, unflinching, and compelling entertainment.

AGUIRRE: WRATH OF GOD

1972

DIRECTOR: Werner Herzog.

SCREENPLAY: Werner Herzog.

CAST: Klaus Kinski, Ruy Guerra, Helena Rojo, Cecilia Rivera.

Color, Not rated (violence), 94m. Subtitled or English versions.

In the 16th century, one of Pizarro's lieutenants leads a small band of conquistadores on a foolhardy quest for El Dorado, the lost city of gold. Kinski gives a remarkable performance as

GREIL MARCUS

Twin Peaks: Fire Walk With Me (1992), directed by David Lynch. Universally panned prequel to the TV series, and Lynch's toughest, cruelest movie. You have to go back to the silent era—and to Lillian Gish—for parallels to what Sheryl Lee does with doomed Laura Palmer. Her performance is heedless, defenseless, and the highest acting in years.

Brute Force (1947), directed by Jules Dassin. Prison-break movie that lives up to its title, with Burt Lancaster baring his teeth and Hume Cronyn baring his black heart.

Across 110th Street (1972), directed by Barry Shear. The most violent, complex, and disturbing of the inner-city Westerns. It should have been called *No Way Out.*

Street of Fire (1984), directed by Walter Hill. A rock 'n' roll fairy tale, with breathtakingly staged performance numbers, a half-decent plot, and career performances by the underrated Michael Paré and the even more underrated Diane Lane. She stands on a stage, miming the impossibly corny "Tonight Is What It Means to Be Young," and it feels like "Like a Rolling Stone" cut with "You Keep Me Hangin' On."

***Symphony for a Massacre** (1965), directed by Jacques Deray. Beginning in Paris, a cabal of crooks fall out—and then, one by one, always to the same ethereal, ghostly musical theme, they fall down. Well-reviewed in its time, this film went right off the map, as if part of its magic was to allow those who saw it to remember it only in dreams.

Greil Marcus is the author of *Mystery Train, Lipstick Traces,* and *Dead Elvis.* He lives in Berkeley.

*This is not yet available on video, but we can hope.

the obsessed madman, Aguirre. Filmed on location in the Peruvian jungles, it's hard to imagine the horrible conditions the actors and crew had to endure and equally hard to believe that Herzog got Kinski to return 10 years later to film *Fitzcarraldo*.

ALIVE

1993

DIRECTOR: Frank Marshall.

SCREENPLAY: John Patrick Shanley, from the book by Piers Paul Read.

CAST: Ethan Hawke, Vincent Spano, Josh Hamilton, Bruce Ramsay, John Haymes Newton, David Kriegel.

Color, R rated, 125m.

The incredible true story of a plane crash in the Andes Mountains during one of the worst winters in many years. Of the 45 passengers and crew, made up mostly of rugby players, 16 survived for 72 days only because they are able to bring themselves to eat the flesh of their friends and family who died. This part of their remarkable story is not sensationalized and the emphasis is on their will to live in a seemingly hopeless situation. Exciting and realistic plane crash sequences. Music by James Newton Howard.

A BETTER TOMORROW

1986

DIRECTOR: John Woo.

SCREENPLAY: Chan Hing Kai, Leung Suk Wah.

CAST: Chow Yun-Fat, Leslie Cheung, Ti Lung.

Color, Not rated (strong violence), 90m. Subtitled or dubbed.

Two brothers, one an idealistic cop, the other a criminal, seek to avenge the murder of their father. Hong Kong-based director Woo manages to combine gloriously excessive gunplay with a sentimental tale of loyalty and friendship, and make it work. Now a highly sought-after action director in the U.S. (*Face/Off, Mission Impossible 2*), this gangster epic is what put him on the map. This is rousing entertainment with a consistent sense of humor. Chow Yun-Fat is very appealing as Mark, a match-chewing gangster with heart.

THE BLACK ARROW

1948

DIRECTOR: Gordon Douglas.

SCREENPLAY: Richard Schayer, David P. Sheppard, Thomas Seller, from the novel by Robert Louis Stevenson.

CAST: Louis Hayward, Janet Blair, George Macready, Edgar Buchanan, Paul Cavanagh.

B&W, Not rated (some violence), 76m.

During the War of the Roses, Sir Richard Shelton sets out to find his father's murderer. Lots of swordplay and a grand finale jousting match are highlights of this little known swashbuckler. Perennial villain George Macready is Shelton's evil uncle who killed his own brother to steal his land.

BLACK ROBE

1991

DIRECTOR: Bruce Beresford.

SCREENPLAY: Brian Moore, from his novel.

CAST: Lothaire Bluteau, August Schellenberg, Aden Young, Sandrine Holt.

Color, R rated, 101m.

In 17th-century Quebec, a young Jesuit missionary (Bluteau) journeys up the St. Lawrence River with Algonquin guides. Believing him to be possessed by demons, his guides desert him, and he continues to his post at the Huron Indian mission alone. The beauty of the Canadian wilderness is captured by cinematographer Peter James, but it's a harsh, unforgiving environment. There's no romanticism in Bruce Beresford's

vision. It's a brutal depiction of unrelenting hardship. The evocative score is by Georges Delerue.

THE BOAT aka DAS BOOT

1981

DIRECTOR: Wolfgang Petersen.

SCREENPLAY: Wolfgang Petersen.

CAST: Jürgen Prochnow, Herbert Grönemeyer, Klaus Wennemann, Hubertus Bengsch.

Color, R rated, 150m. In German with English subtitles or dubbed.

A German U-boat during WW II is the setting for this vivid picture of the grim, claustrophobic terror of life aboard a submarine at war. Probably the best movie about submarine life ever made, it conveys an atmosphere of suffocating, sweating dread. The life expectancy was short for these crews. This highly suspenseful, realistic account of war at sea was, at the time it was made, the most expensive movie ever produced in Germany at $12 million. Nominated for six Academy Awards.

CAPRICORN ONE

1978

DIRECTOR: Peter Hyams.

SCREENPLAY: Peter Hyams.

CAST: Elliott Gould, James Brolin, Brenda Vaccaro, Hal Holbrook, Sam Waterston, Karen Black, O. J. Simpson, Telly Savalas.

Color, PG rated, 123m.

Because the premise of this movie is that the first manned flight to Mars is a hoax, it's usually classified as science fiction, and underrated. But, at heart, this is an action movie centering on the ill-fated astronauts Brolin, Waterston, and Simpson, who are forced to go along with the hoax to protect their families. When it becomes evident that they're expendable, the supposed victims of a reentry accident, they try to escape. Elliott Gould is a reporter who smells something is wrong, and goes after the story. Loaded with chases by planes, helicopters, and cars. Jerry Goldsmith provides the score.

CASUALTIES OF WAR

1989

DIRECTOR: Brian De Palma.

SCREENPLAY: David Rabe, from the book by Daniel Lang.

CAST: Michael J. Fox, Sean Penn, Don Harvey, John C. Reilly, John Leguizamo, Thuy Thu Le.

Color, R rated, 113m.

This fact-based drama about the rape and murder of a peasant girl by American soldiers on patrol in Vietnam was a change of pace for both its director and its star. Michael J. Fox gives a strong performance as the soldier who refuses to take part in the crime and eventually forces the Army to bring the other four men in his squad to trial, despite threats and harassment. A harrowing, but hopeful account of an incident that was reported in *The New Yorker* on October 18, 1969.

CHARLEY VARRICK

1973

DIRECTOR: Don Siegel.

SCREENPLAY: Howard Rodman, Dean Reisner, from the novel *The Looters* by John Reese.

CAST: Walter Matthau, Joe Don Baker, Felicia Farr, Andy Robinson, John Vernon.

Color, PG rated, 111m.

Matthau, in an efficient, straight performance, plays a small-time crop duster/bank robber who discovers that he's inadvertently stolen laundered Mafia money from a local bank. The fun is trying to figure out how he's going to get away with it. Joe Don Baker is the hit man hired to find him, and Sheree North appears in a small role as a photographer. This is the first of three excellent crime-related straight roles for Matthau in the early '70s (the other two being *The Laughing Policeman* and *The Taking of Pelham 1,2,3*).

THE CRIMSON PIRATE

1952

DIRECTOR: Robert Siodmak.

SCREENPLAY: Roland Kibbee.

CAST: Burt Lancaster, Nick Cravat, Eva Bartok, Torin Thatcher, Christopher Lee.

Color, Not rated, 104m.

They don't get much better than this comedy swashbuckler featuring Burt Lancaster in great shape and brilliant technicolor. Lancaster and his lifelong pal, Nick Cravat, display the high-flying acrobatic skills they developed as circus performers in this tale of pirate doings in the Mediterranean. This rousing adventure was released the same year that Lancaster established himself as a dramatic actor in *Come Back Little Sheba.*

THE FLAME AND THE ARROW

1950

DIRECTOR: Jacques Tourneur.

SCREENPLAY: Waldo Salt.

CAST: Burt Lancaster, Virginia Mayo, Robert Douglas, Aline MacMahon, Frank Allenby, Nick Cravat.

Color, Not rated, 88m.

What's not to love in this exciting adventure full of amazing stunts, colorful costumes and a rousing Max Steiner score. Set in 16th-century Lombardy, Italy, it's the tale of an outlaw (Lancaster) who leads a band of freedom fighters to rid their home of evil German invaders. Rip-roaring fun, in the spirit of the great Douglas Fairbanks swashbucklers.

GO TELL THE SPARTANS

1978

DIRECTOR: Ted Post.

SCREENPLAY: Wendell Mayes, from the novel *Incident at Muc Wa* by Daniel Ford.

CAST: Burt Lancaster, Craig Wasson, Marc Singer, Jonathan Goldsmith, Dennis Howard.

Color, R rated, 114m.

Lancaster gives an effectively subdued performance as the cynical, weary "advisory group commander" of an Army camp in Vietnam in 1964, during the early years of U.S. involvement. This straightforward account of a rescue mission into the jungle led by ambitious young officer Wasson is one of the best, and most realistic, of the movies set during the Vietnam war. Unfortunately, it was overshadowed by the epics of the late 1970s (*Apocalypse Now, The Deer Hunter*).

HARD-BOILED

1992

DIRECTOR: John Woo.

SCREENPLAY: Barry Wong, from a story by John Woo.

CAST: Chow Yun-Fat, Tony Leung, Teresa Mo, Philip Chan.

Color, Not rated (profanity, strong violence), 126m. Available subtitled or dubbed.

Chow Yun-Fat is Tequila, a renegade cop out to stop a ring of gun smugglers with the aid of hit man Leung. Once again, John Woo has created an exhilarating action-thriller

crammed with such outrageous overkill that by the end there's nothing left to blow up. His use of color, slow-motion and sound create gun battles that have a signature dreamlike quality.

THE HIDDEN FORTRESS

1958

DIRECTOR: Akira Kurosawa.

SCREENPLAY: Akira Kurosawa, Hideo Oguni, Ryuzo Kikushima, Shinobu Hoshimoto.

CAST: Toshiro Mifune, Misa Uehara, Takashi Shimura, Susumu Fujita, Eiko Miyoshi.

B&W, Not rated, 139m. Subtitled.

During civil wars in medieval Japan, a general (Mifune) escorts a deposed princess and her family gold to safe territory. Two bumbling peasants, greedy for the gold, tag along. George Lucas acknowledges that this comedy-adventure was the inspiration for *Star Wars,* with Alec Guinness in the Mifune role, Carrie Fisher as the strong-willed princess, and R2D2 and C3PO as the comic sidekicks played by Minoru Chiaki and Kamatari Fujiwara. This is light-weight fare, full of humor, great scenery, and spectacular stunts.

THE HIT

1984

DIRECTOR: Stephen Frears.

SCREENPLAY: Peter Prince.

CAST: Terence Stamp, John Hurt, Tim Roth, Laura del Sol.

Color, R rated, 98m.

Methodical Hurt and loose-cannon Roth are sent to Spain to dispose of Stamp, a stool pigeon who moved to Spain for protection after he testified against his gangster bosses in England. What they find, in a new twist on the hit man story, is an apparently willing victim who cheerfully accompanies them on the road to Paris to meet his fate. This is a fresh take on an old story, with interesting characters and surprises along the way. Hurt, Roth, and Stamp are all sensational. Roth and Hurt were reunited in two more wicked roles in *Rob Roy* (1995). Eric Clapton plays the guitar music of Paco de Lucia on the soundtrack.

THE KILLER

1989

DIRECTOR: John Woo.

SCREENPLAY: John Woo.

CAST: Chow Yun-Fat, Danny Lee, Sally Yeh, Chu Kong.

Color, R rated, 110m. Available dubbed or in Cantonese with subtitles.

Chow Yun-Fat is a hit man on the verge of retirement who accidentally blinds a young woman during a gun battle. Consumed with guilt, he agrees to one last job to pay for an operation to restore her sight, and ends up wanted by both the police and the mob. Ultraviolent to absurdity, but with great acting and a very sentimental nature, this visually stunning John Woo masterpiece will take your breath away and leave you giddy. Don't miss it!

THE LAST AMERICAN HERO
aka **HARD DRIVER**

1973

DIRECTOR: Lamont Johnson.

SCREENPLAY: William Roberts, based on articles by Tom Wolfe.

CAST: Jeff Bridges, Valerie Perrine, Geraldine Fitzgerald, Art Lund, Ned Beatty, Gary Busey.

Color, PG rated, 95m.

Race car driver Bridges starts his career running bootleg whiskey for his father. After his dad lands in jail, Bridges enters a demolition derby and ultimately becomes a stock car racing champion. The fine cast includes Art Lund as his moonshiner dad, and Geraldine Fitzgerald as his feisty mom. Based on a series of articles on the life of North Carolina stock car legend Junior Johnson, written by Tom Wolfe. A good-natured, fast-paced story with a strong performance by Bridges.

EL MARIACHI

1992

DIRECTOR: Robert Rodriguez.

SCREENPLAY: Robert Rodriguez.

CAST: Carlos Gallardo, Consuelo Gomez, Reinol Martinez, Peter Marquandt.

Color, R rated, 81m. Available dubbed or subtitled.

This violent tongue-in-cheek picture turns on a case of mistaken identity. Gunman Azul, who carries his weapons in a guitar case, seeks revenge on drug dealer Moco, who has double-crossed him. Enter a mariachi singer with a guitar case who is mistaken for Azul by Moco's men and has to find a way out alive. Peter Marquandt does a menacing turn à la Christopher Walken as the drug dealer Moco. The lively soundtrack is complete with cartoon sound effects. This low- budget wonder made for $7,000 puts the megabuck action movies to shame.

A MIDNIGHT CLEAR

1992

DIRECTOR: Keith Gordon.

SCREENPLAY: Keith Gordon, from the novel by William Wharton.

CAST: Peter Berg, Kevin Dillon, Arye Gross, Ethan Hawke, Gary Sinise.

Color, R rated, 107m.

It's Christmas, and World War II is winding down. A U.S. intelligence unit is sent to a remote cottage near enemy territory to report on German troop movements. When they discover a motley group of very old and very young German soldiers in the area, they attempt to fashion their own peace in order to survive the last few months of the war. This impressive, but little known follow-up to Gordon's first feature, *The Chocolate War,* is an unusually satisfying war movie. Score by Mark Isham.

MOUNTAINS OF THE MOON

1989

DIRECTOR:	Bob Rafelson.
SCREENPLAY:	William Harrison, Bob Rafelson, from the book *Burton and Speke* by William Harrison.
CAST:	Patrick Bergin, Iain Glen, Richard E. Grant, Fiona Shaw, John Savident, James Villiers, Adrian Rawlins.

Color, R rated, 136m.

Director Rafelson indulges his own taste for adventurous travel is this compelling account of the expeditions of 19th-century British explorers Richard Burton and John Hanning Speke in search of the source of the Nile. Based on the biographical novel by William Harrison as well as the journals of the two men, this is a compelling account of their explorations in Africa and their eventual parting of ways. A strong evocation of time and place add to this good old-fashioned adventure.

NAKED PREY

1966

DIRECTOR: Cornel Wilde.

SCREENPLAY: Clint Johnston, Don Peters.

CAST: Cornel Wilde, Gert Van Den Berg, Ken Gampu.

Color, Not rated (violence), 94m.

In 1840, while on safari in Africa, hunter Wilde is captured by a hostile tribe and forced to watch his companions be tortured and killed. He is stripped, given a head start, and hunted like a wild animal. Wilde's own company produced this unusual and brutal tale of survival.

ONE FALSE MOVE

1992

DIRECTOR: Carl Franklin.

SCREENPLAY: Billy Bob Thornton, Tom Epperson.

CAST: Bill Paxton, Cynda Williams, Billy Bob Thornton, Michael Beach, Jim Metzler, Earl Billings, Natalie Canerday, Robert Ginnaven, Robert Anthony Bell, Kevin Hunter.

Color, R rated, 105m.

Three drug dealers are on the run from L.A. to rural Arkansas. Don't be deterred by the extreme violence of the first ten minutes, and you'll be rewarded with a well-written, intelligent movie that avoids clichés. It's brimming with detail and the local flavor of a small Arkansas town and its people. Bill Paxton is convincing as Sheriff Dale "Hurricane" Dixon who has to deal with the arrogance of big-city cops who show up in pursuit of the drug dealers. A first-rate directing debut for Franklin.

THE PACKAGE

1989

DIRECTOR: Andrew Davis.

SCREENPLAY: John Bishop.

CAST: Gene Hackman, Joanna Cassidy, Tommy Lee Jones, Dennis Franz, Reni Santori, John Heard.

Color, R rated, 108m.

Career Army sergeant Hackman is escorting prisoner Jones from Berlin to Washington, D.C. for a court-martial when Jones escapes and Hackman finds himself in the middle of a conspiracy made up of disenchanted American and Soviet military officers. This violent, taut thriller didn't make it at the box office, but it boasts strong performances from Hackman in the lead, Jones as a paid assassin, and Heard as one of the conspirators. Effectively done by former cinematographer Davis, who's scored his biggest commercial successes in the action genre with Steven Seagal (*Above the Law, Under Siege*) and the huge 1993 hit *The Fugitive*.

PATHFINDER

1987

DIRECTOR: Nils Gaup.

SCREENPLAY: Nils Gaup.

CAST: Mikkel Gaup, Nils Utsi, Svein Scharffenberg, Helgi Skulason.

Color, Not rated (violence), 86m. Subtitled.

Based on a Lapp folk tale, there is very little dialogue in this nonstop adventure filmed in the snowy north of Norway. A teenage boy whose family is murdered by a ruthless band of criminals is captured and forced to lead the thugs to a coastal village that they intend to pillage. This brutal, direct, and fascinating film was nominated for a Best Foreign Film Oscar. The brave young man is played by the director's son.

POINT BLANK

1967

DIRECTOR: John Boorman.

SCREENPLAY: Alexander Jacobs, David Newhouse, Rafe Newhouse, from the novel *The Hunter* by Richard Stark.

CAST: Lee Marvin, Angie Dickinson, Keenan Wynn, Carroll O'Connor, Lloyd Bochner, Michael Strong.

Color, Not rated (violence), 92m.

After being shot and left for dead on Alcatraz Island by his unfaithful wife and double-dealing partner, Marvin recovers and sets out for revenge. Though it was dismissed in 1967, this influential and stylish thriller features one of Marvin's best performances. Boorman and Marvin worked together again the following year on *Hell in the Pacific.*

PRIME CUT

1972

DIRECTOR: Michael Ritchie.

SCREENPLAY: Robert Dillon.

CAST: Lee Marvin, Gene Hackman, Gregory Walcott, Sissy Spacek, Angel Tompkins.

Color, R rated, 86m.

The opening sequence in a slaughterhouse sets the tone for this gritty, nasty, and funny movie. Lee Marvin is an enforcer from Chicago who goes reluctantly to Kansas City to put Hackman (Mary Ann, of Mary Ann's Meats) in line. Mary Ann, who's been managing a narcotics and white slavery business on the side, is about as despicable a character as you're likely to find. Marvin seems to be in a perpetual state of irritation. This was Spacek's first film.

THE RIGHT STUFF

1983

DIRECTOR: Philip Kaufman.

SCREENPLAY: Philip Kaufman, from the book by Tom Wolfe.

CAST: Sam Shepard, Scott Glenn, Ed Harris, Dennis Quaid, Fred Ward, Barbara Hershey, Kim Stanley, Veronica Cartwright, Pamela Reed, Harry Shearer.

Color, PG rated, 193m.

It's a shame that this boisterous account of America's early space program was a flop at the box office because it's bursting with broad comedy, great performances and stunning recreations of space flight. It's an epic adventure and a biting satire on American culture put together with an exhilarating, Oscar-winning score by Bill Conti.

RUNAWAY TRAIN

1985

DIRECTOR: Andrei Konchalovsky.

SCREENPLAY: Djordje Milicevic, Paul Zindel, Edward Bunker, from a screenplay by Akira Kurosawa.

CAST: Jon Voight, Eric Roberts, Rebecca DeMornay, Kyle T. Heffner.

Color, R rated, 111m.

Everybody loves a good locomotive and this movie's got one, and much more. Voight and Roberts were both nominated for Oscars for their roles as escaped prisoners trapped on a runaway train in the Alaskan wilderness. Rebecca DeMornay is also strong in a supporting role. Roaring entertainment from beginning to end.

THE SAMURAI TRILOGY PART I: MUSASHI MIYAMOTO

1954

DIRECTOR: Hiroshi Inagaki.

SCREENPLAY: Tokuhei Wakao, Hiroshi Inagaki, from the novel *Musashi* by Eiji Yoshikawa.

CAST: Toshiro Mifune, Kaoru Yachigusa, Rentaro Mikuni, Mariko Okada.

Color, Not rated, 97m. Subtitled.

This Academy Award winner for Best Foreign Language Film of 1955 follows the formative years of legendary Japanese swordsman Musashi Miyamoto. As a young man he leaves his village to go to war with dreams of becoming a samurai, only to return in defeat as an outlaw. He then starts his training with his Buddhist monk mentor while Otsu, the woman who loves him, waits patiently for his return. A beautifully photographed and touching story.

THE SAMURAI TRILOGY PART II: DUEL AT ICHIJOJI TEMPLE

1956

DIRECTOR: Hiroshi Inagaki.

SCREENPLAY: Tokuhei Wakao, Hiroshi Inagaki, from the novel *Musashi* by Eiji Yoshikawa.

CAST: Toshiro Mifune, Koji Tsuruta, Sachio Sakai, Akihiko Hirata, Kaoru Yachigusa, Mariko Okada.

Color, Not rated, 107m. Subtitled.

In this sequel, Musashi continues his travels, developing his skills, looking for wisdom. Otsu still waits, as does Akemi, but he has given up the love of women. Great swordplay in the rice paddies. Again, beautifully filmed, but with a darker, more moody atmosphere than Part I.

THE SAMURAI TRILOGY PART III: DUEL AT GANRYU ISLAND

1956

DIRECTOR: Hiroshi Inagaki.

SCREENPLAY: Tokuhei Wakao, Hiroshi Inagaki, from the novel *Musashi* by Eiji Yoshikawa.

CAST: Toshiro Mifune, Kaoru Yachigusa, Mariko Okada.

Color, Not rated, 105m. Subtitled.

The final chapter of Musashi's story opens with a dazzling view of a cascading waterfall. Musashi helps defend a small farming village against marauding brigands. His reputation as a swordsman has traveled, and the story builds to a final duel in the setting sun with his archrival Kojiro. His spiritual quest and physical training have led him to the principles of honor, duty, and respect for his opponents in battle. These three colorful films are best seen in sequence, but they can also be enjoyed independently.

SCARAMOUCHE

1952

DIRECTOR: George Sidney.

SCREENPLAY: Ronald Millar, George Froeschel, based on the novel by Rafael Sabatini.

CAST: Stewart Granger, Eleanor Parker, Janet Leigh, Mel Ferrer.

Color, Not rated, 111m.

Granger is at his best in this 18th-century swashbuckler. He's in pursuit of the villainous Marquis (Ferrer), who has killed his friend in a sword fight. The final duel is the longest in film history. The sets, costumes, and scenery are all a bonus.

SOLDIER OF ORANGE

1979

DIRECTOR: Paul Verhoeven.

SCREENPLAY: Paul Verhoeven.

CAST: Rutger Hauer, Jeroen Krabbé, Peter Faber, Derek De Lint, Eddy Habbema.

Color, R rated, 165m.

After the Netherlands were invaded by the Nazis in 1940, a group of aristocratic college students caught up in the war effort join the Dutch resistance movement. The title refers to the House of Orange, the Netherlands' royal government, which was exiled after the invasion. A brilliant, exciting war story with atmosphere and good period detail, it also brought Hauer international attention. Director Verhoeven is best known in the U.S. for *Basic Instinct* (1992).

SORCERER

1977

DIRECTOR: William Friedkin.

SCREENPLAY: Walon Green.

CAST: Roy Scheider, Bruno Cremer, Francisco Rabal, Amidou, Ramon Bieri, Peter Capell.

Color, R rated, 122m.

This action-packed remake of *The Wages of Fear* was not well received by critics or moviegoers when it was first released. A thriller about an American fugitive (Scheider) who takes a job transporting nitroglycerine across nearly impassable jungle terrain in Latin America, it has some astonishing scenes, including trucks crossing a dilapidated suspension bridge in a driving rainstorm. He may as well have descended into Hell. The dynamic score is by Tangerine Dream.

THE STEEL HELMET

1951

DIRECTOR: Samuel Fuller.

SCREENPLAY: Samuel Fuller.

CAST: Gene Evans, Robert Hutton, James Edwards, Steve Brodie, Richard Loo.

B&W, Not rated, 84m.

Evans is a battle-worn sergeant who escapes from a North Korean P.O.W. camp early in the Korean War. He joins up with other American soldiers cut off from their units. Dazzling action sequences, especially when Evans tracks down an enemy sniper. This is an impressive achievement on a small budget for producer-writer-director Fuller.

THIS GUN FOR HIRE

1942

DIRECTOR: Frank Tuttle.

SCREENPLAY: Albert Maltz, W. R. Burnett, from *A Gun for Sale* by Graham Greene.

CAST: Alan Ladd, Veronica Lake, Robert Preston, Laird Cregar, Tully Marshall.

B&W, Not rated, 81m.

In the role that made him a lead actor, Alan Ladd is Raven, a cold-hearted killer whose only soft spot is for stray cats. He's a paid gunman who is cheated out of his fee for a hit and seeks revenge on the guy who double-crossed him. Veronica Lake is a "singing magician" he meets along the way. This perverse adaptation of a Graham Greene spy-thriller has enough plot turns and twists to keep it more interesting than most in the genre.

THE TRAIN

1965

DIRECTOR: John Frankenheimer.

SCREENPLAY: Franklin Coen, Frank Davis.

CAST: Burt Lancaster, Paul Scofield, Jeanne Moreau, Michel Simon.

B&W, Not rated, 133m.

1944 occupied France is the setting for this gripping adventure about a Nazi, Scofield, who's consumed with moving French art treasures secretly to Germany on a special train before the Allies take Paris. Lancaster is a resistance leader who reluctantly gets involved in trying to stop the train. Loaded with action, unrelenting suspense and superb acting, especially by Scofield as the obsessed Nazi officer who refuses to give up. A smooth Maurice Jarre score.

TRESPASS

1992

DIRECTOR: Walter Hill.

SCREENPLAY: Bob Gale, Robert Zemeckis.

CAST: Bill Paxton, Ice T, William Sadler, Ice Cube, Art Evans, De'Voreaux White.

Color, R rated, 101m.

This variation on *The Treasure of the Sierra Madre* is set in an abandoned inner-city warehouse, where Paxton and pal Sadler go looking for stolen gold treasure that's rumored to be hidden there. But unfortunately for them, they're violating the turf of drug lords Ice T and Ice Cube. What ensues is a gunfire fest. Director Hill gives us one of his best movies with this violent, surprisingly funny thriller. The exciting score is by Ry Cooder.

TRUE ROMANCE

1993

DIRECTOR: Tony Scott.

SCREENPLAY: Quentin Tarantino.

CAST: Christian Slater, Patricia Arquette, Dennis Hopper, Gary Oldman, Brad Pitt, Christopher Walken, Val Kilmer, Bronson Pinchot, Michael Rapaport, Saul Rubinek, Chris Penn, Tom Sizemore, Samuel L. Jackson.

Color, R rated, 118m. (Unrated version also available on video, 120m.)

This funny, violent free-for-all features Slater and Arquette as young lovers on the run from bad guy extraordinaire Christopher Walken. Many memorable scenes, but standouts are Walken attempting to extract information from defiant father Dennis Hopper and an outrageous standoff in a posh hotel suite. Lots of great acting in small but juicy parts, including a hilarious Brad Pitt as a singularly laid-back roommate. Music by Hans Zimmer.

UTU

1983

DIRECTOR: Geoff Murphy.

SCREENPLAY: Geoff Murphy, Keith Aberdein.

CAST: Anzac Wallace, Bruno Lawrence, Tim Elliott, Kelly Johnson, Wi Kuki Kaa.

Color, R rated, 104m.

In 1870 New Zealand, a defiant Maori tribesman (Wallace) sets out to eradicate the British settlers after his family and village are wiped out by the army. He becomes a guerilla leader, mocking and taunting the British even as he exacts Utu (Maori for revenge). Enhanced by the spectacular mountain setting, this is a violent, darkly funny film. Music by

John Charles, performed on a traditional Maori flute with the New Zealand Symphony.

A WALK IN THE SUN

1946

DIRECTOR: Lewis Milestone.

SCREENPLAY: Robert Rossen, from the novel by Harry Brown.

CAST: Dana Andrews, Richard Conte, Sterling Holloway, John Ireland, George Tyne, Herbert Rudley, Richard Benedict, Norman Lloyd, Lloyd Bridges, Huntz Hall.

B&W, Not rated, 117m.

There's plenty of combat in this World War II account set during the invasion of Salerno in 1943. But the emphasis here is on the psychological aspects of combat for a small unit of veteran soldiers on one critical morning. Not flashy, but well written and acted. An effective war movie.

THE WHITE DAWN

1974

DIRECTOR: Philip Kaufman.

SCREENPLAY: James Houston, Tom Rickman, from a novel by Houston.

CAST: Warren Oates, Lou Gossett Jr., Timothy Bottoms, an Eskimo cast.

Color, PG rated, 109m.

At the turn of the century, three survivors from a whaling ship are rescued and cared for by a group of Eskimos. Bottoms is friendly and outgoing, Gossett is suspicious, and Oates is downright hostile. Their presence causes major disruptions in the lives of their hosts, some life-threatening. Full of detail about the difficult and sometimes brutal existence of the Eskimos, this is a fascinating tale. The powerful score is by Henry Mancini.

WHITE HEAT

1949

DIRECTOR: Raoul Walsh.

SCREENPLAY: Ivan Goff, Ben Roberts, from a story by Virginia Kellogg.

CAST: James Cagney, Virginia Mayo, Edmond O'Brien, Fred Clark, Margaret Wycherly.

B&W, Not rated, 114m.

Cagney gives one of his best performances as Cody Jarrett, a murderous, psychotic gangster plagued by excruciating headaches and a mother fixation. His Ma (Wycherly) is a tough cookie, too. Mayo is his adulterous wife. Fast-paced action is highlighted by car chases, prison escape, gunplay and an explosive finale at an oil refinery. In the tradition of the '30s gangster movies, but at a new, shocking level of violence.

WHO'LL STOP THE RAIN?

1978

DIRECTOR: Karel Reisz.

SCREENPLAY: Judidth Rascoe, Robert Stone, from his novel *Dog Soldiers.*

CAST: Nick Nolte, Tuesday Weld, Michael Moriarty, Anthony Zerbe, Richard Masur, Ray Sharkey.

Color, R rated, 126m.

Vietnam vet Moriarty convinces his Navy pal Nolte to smuggle heroin from Vietnam to the U.S., but what neither of them knows is that they're being set up. Nolte and Moriarty's wife (Weld) are forced to hide out from the ruthless Zerbe and his cohorts, who are looking for the heroin. Nolte and Weld are outstanding as the unfortunate pawns in this dirty game.

WILD AT HEART

1990

DIRECTOR: David Lynch.

SCREENPLAY: David Lynch.

CAST: Nicolas Cage, Laura Dern, Diane Ladd, Willem Dafoe, Isabella Rossellini, Harry Dean Stanton, Crispin Glover.

Color, R rated, 127m.

Lynch indulges his penchant for whacked-out low-life characters in this romantic-comedy road picture on speed. Most notable in this smorgasbord of psychos is Willem Dafoe as the revolting Bobby Peru, one of the slimiest, most malevolent characters ever to appear on film. Visually stunning, with Lynch's trademark industrial-park sound design, *Wild at Heart* is recommended for those who take their humor black.

YOJIMBO

1961

DIRECTOR: Akira Kurosawa.

SCREENPLAY: Ryuzo Kikushima, Akira Kurosawa.

CAST: Toshiro Mifune, Takashi Shimura, Eijiro Tono, Iko Sawamura, Seizaburo Kawazu.

B&W, Not rated, 110m. Subtitled.

In 1860 Japan, an unemployed samurai (Mifune) sees an opportunity to make some money by hiring himself out to both sides in a local dispute. Kurosawa's love of American Westerns shows in the dramatic showdowns between rival gangs on the wide, dusty main street that looks more like Dodge City than rural Japan. The rambunctious score by Masaru Sato blends perfectly with the narrative. This wry epic was the inspiration for Sergio Leone's spaghetti Western cycle that started with *A Fistful of Dollars*.

ZULU

1964

DIRECTOR: Cy Endfield.

SCREENPLAY: John Prebble, Cy Endfield.

CAST: Stanley Baker, Jack Hawkins, Michael Caine, Ulla Jacobsson, James Booth, Nigel Green.

Color, Not rated, 135m.

Spectacular battle scenes are the highlight of this fact-based story about the 1879 attack by Zulu warriors on the undermanned British post at Rorke's Drift in South Africa. Scenes of the Zulu preparations for battle are also superb. Stanley Baker and Michael Caine (in his first major screen role) are impressive. An old-fashioned, grand-scale epic adventure.

A. E. HOTCHNER

One-Eyed Jacks (1961), directed by Marlon Brando.

Betrayal (1962), directed by David Jones.

The Left-handed Gun (1958), directed by Arthur Penn.

Baby Doll (1956), directed by Elia Kazan.

The Good, The Bad and The Ugly (1966), directed by Sergio Leone.

A. E. Hotchner is the author of *Papa Hemingway,* and the novels *King of the Hill* and *Louisiana Purchase.* He lives in New York.

Comedy

ALL NIGHT LONG

1981

DIRECTOR:	Jean-Claude Tramont.
SCREENPLAY:	W. D. Richter.
CAST:	Gene Hackman, Barbra Streisand, Diane Ladd, Dennis Quaid, Kevin Dobson, William Daniels, Ann Doran.

Color, R rated, 88m.

This slightly loopy comedy stars a very likable Gene Hackman as an executive who's demoted to night manager at a drugstore after blowing off steam at his bosses. Restless and bored with his life, he starts an affair with his neighbor's ditsy wife (Streisand), who is already having an affair with his dim son (Quaid). He eventually drops out of workaday life altogether when he decides to become an inventor. A very satisfying comedy anchored by Hackman's delightful performance.

AVANTI!

1972

DIRECTOR:	Billy Wilder.
SCREENPLAY:	Billy Wilder, I. A. L. Diamond, from the play by Samuel Taylor.
CAST:	Jack Lemmon, Juliet Mills, Clive Revill, Edward Andrews, Gianfranco Barra.

Color, R rated, 144m.

When stodgy businessman Lemmon goes to Italy to claim his dead father's body, he surprises himself by falling for the luscious daughter of his late father's mistress. This typically sardonic Billy Wilder black comedy is blessed with fine performances and lovely scenery.

BAGDAD CAFE

1988

DIRECTOR: Percy Adlon.

SCREENPLAY: Percy Adlon, Eleonore Adlon, Christopher Doherty.

CAST: Marianne Sägebrecht, Jack Palance, CCH Pounder, Christine Kaufmann, Monica Calhoun, Darron Flagg.

Color, PG rated, 108m.

In the remote California desert, plump German tourist Sägebrecht gets dumped off at the Bagdad Cafe and Motel where she joins the motley group of misfits who hang out there. The quirkiest of this oddball bunch is Jack Palance. He nearly steals the show as a former Hollywood set decorator-turned-eccentric-painter who becomes obsessed with doing her portrait. Another funny, touching performance from Sägebrecht, who also stars in Adlon's *Sugarbaby* and *Rosalie Goes Shopping.*

BARFLY

1987

DIRECTOR: Barbet Schroeder.

SCREENPLAY: Charles Bukowski.

CAST: Mickey Rourke, Faye Dunaway, Alice Krige, J. C. Quinn, Frank Stallone.

Color, R rated, 100m.

You can almost smell the stale cigarettes and booze at the Golden Horn bar where writer Rourke spends his days. He's happily down and out, and he becomes even happier when he

CHARLIE HAAS

Avanti! (1972), directed by Billy Wilder. Wilder and Diamond, still going strong in the early '70s, make a gorgeous, witty romantic comedy with Jack Lemmon and Juliet Mills. Key moment: Clive Revill explains the Italian lunch hour to Lemmon.

So Fine (1981). Some of my fellow Andrew Bergman fans may have missed this one. Key moment: Jack Warden commends Ryan O'Neal on his growing grasp of Yiddish.

Funnybones. This will probably be on other lists, so I'll just add my vote. Key moment: Lee Evans's pantomime act to radio tape collage.

Bottle Rocket. Everyone read the recent success fable in the papers: young guys in Texas write the script on spec, shoot the first 10 pages on a shoestring, take the script and reel to Sundance, get a deal at Columbia and make the movie, doing their own directing and starring. Almost nobody saw the movie, though, because the studio only semireleased it. No one key moment, but the eccentric structure and the way these guys talk to one another shouldn't be missed.

Love Potion #9 (1992). Not a complete success, but no Dale Launer movie deserves such a cursory release. Key moment: the larval Sandra Bullock decides to keep the car manufacturer's necklace.

Charlie Haas, the beliked American humorist and screenwriter, lives in Oakland, California.

meets soulmate Dunaway. Rourke and Dunaway create memorable characters who manage to be both hilarious and pathetic. This tale of alcoholism and irresponsibility is told with insight by Bukowski, who undoubtedly has been there.

BAXTER

1991

DIRECTOR: Jerome Boivin.

SCREENPLAY: Jacques Audiard, Jerome Boivin.

CAST: Lise Delarmare, Jean Mercure, Jacques Spiesser, Catherine Ferran.

Color, Not rated (profanity, violence, nudity), 85m. Subtitled.

A bull terrier named Baxter narrates most of this horror-comedy. Shuttled from one home to another, Baxter finds some joy, but mostly frustration. He vents his rage against his clueless owners in devious and sometimes fatal ways. He longs to find someone who is just like him, who doesn't feel love or fear. He gets more than he bargained for when he ends up with a kid who's fascinated by Hitler's last days with Eva Braun. This wildly original production makes superb use of music to create an air of impending doom.

BILLY LIAR

1963

DIRECTOR: John Schlesinger.

SCREENPLAY: Keith Waterhouse, Willis Hall.

CAST: Tom Courtenay, Julie Christie, Wilfred Pickles, Ethel Griffies, Mona Washbourne.

B&W, Not rated, 98m.

In working-class England, dreams are no doubt what keep some people going, but young Billy's fantasy life interferes with his ability to carry on normally. Julie Christie, in her first major role, encourages Billy to run away with her to London. And what man in his right mind wouldn't? Courtenay creates a very engaging character in this winsome comedy-drama.

THE BLISS OF MRS. BLOSSOM

1968

DIRECTOR: Joseph McGrath.

SCREENPLAY: Alec Coppel, Denis Norden.

CAST: Shirley MacLaine, Richard Attenborough, James Booth, Freddie Jones, Bob Monkhouse, John Cleese.

Color, M/PG rated, 93m.

Attenborough is the busy owner of a brassiere manufacturing company who likes to play symphony conductor in front of his stereo at home, and MacLaine is his happy wife with a flair for interior decorating. Booth comes to the house to repair her sewing machine, becomes her lover, and moves into the attic for five years without Attenborough's knowledge. This frothy sex farce is full of twists and hilarious small roles, including Jones as a bumbling detective, Monkhouse as a psychiatrist, and John Cleese as a store clerk. The dazzling set design has to be seen to be appreciated.

BOUDU SAVED FROM DROWNING

1932

DIRECTOR: Jean Renoir.

SCREENPLAY: Jean Renoir.

CAST: Michel Simon, Charles Granval, Marcelle Hania, Jean Dasté.

B&W, Not rated, 87m. Subtitled.

This wonderful film is far superior to its popular remake *Down and Out in Beverly Hills*. Boudu is a tramp who attempts suicide by jumping into the Seine, but he's rescued by a well-meaning bookseller and his family who vainly attempt to civilize him. He's more interested in taking what they give him and living free and unfettered, doing whatever strikes his fancy. Michel Simon is thoroughly believable as the defiantly unredeemable Boudu.

THE CAPTAIN'S PARADISE

1953

DIRECTOR: Anthony Kimmins.

SCREENPLAY: Alec Coppel, Nicholas Phipps.

CAST: Alec Guinness, Yvonne De Carlo, Celia Johnson, Bill Fraser, Peter Bull.

B&W, Not rated, 77m.

As a ferry captain, the great Alec Guinness merrily crosses the Strait of Gibraltar between his two wives, thinking he has the best of everything. He sees himself as the sophisticated, worldly mariner. His English wife (Johnson) is quiet and correct in every way, and his Moroccan wife (De Carlo) is joyous and flamboyant. But no scheme is perfect, and he eventually gets careless, with hilarious consequences. The movie received an Oscar nomination for Best Original Story (Coppel).

CHAMELEON STREET

1991

DIRECTOR: Wendell B. Harris, Jr.

SCREENPLAY: Wendell B. Harris, Jr.

CAST: Wendell B. Harris, Jr., Angela Leslie, Amina Fakir.

Color, R rated, 95m.

Harris wrote, directed and starred in this biting comedy based on the true story of William Douglas Street, Jr., a black man who was able to successfully impersonate an exchange student, reporter, surgeon, and lawyer because of his uncanny ability to intuit what other people need and to become it. Harris's witty dialogue and narration create a potent commentary on what it's like to be a black man in our society. This little-known work deserves a bigger audience.

CHAMPAGNE FOR CAESAR

1950

DIRECTOR: Richard B. Whorf.

SCREENPLAY: Hans Jacoby, Fred Brady.

CAST: Ronald Colman, Vincent Price, Celeste Holm, Barbara Britton, Art Linkletter.

B&W, Not rated, 99m.

Colman is Beauregard Bottomley, a self-proclaimed genius and unemployed stuffed shirt. He's turned down for a job at the Milady Soap Co. because he offends the eccentric president of the company, Burnbridge Waters (Price), who doesn't like intellectuals or humor. Colman decides to go on the "Masquerade for Money" quiz show, sponsored by Milady, and bankrupt the show by winning all the assets of the company. The entire cast is delightful, especially Price as the "High Lama of Lather." This intelligent skewering of quiz shows, TV, and the corporate world is just as relevant today. Great fun.

CHAN IS MISSING

1982

DIRECTOR: Wayne Wang.

SCREENPLAY: Wayne Wang, Isaac Cronin, Terrel Seltzer.

CAST: Wood Moy, Marc Hayashi, Laureen Chew, Juki Nihei, Peter Wang.

B&W, Not rated (profanity), 80m.

In San Francisco's Chinatown, a Chinese-American cabbie and his obnoxious nephew, Steve, go looking for Chan, another cabbie, who has disappeared with some of their money. In the course of their search they have hilarious conversations about the differences between their generations and other issues of the day. This comedy-drama-mystery cost only $20,000 to make and was Wang's first feature. Wang is best known for the highly successful *The Joy Luck Club*, and his most recent films are *Anywhere but Here* and *Center of the World.*

CHILLY SCENES OF WINTER
aka **HEAD OVER HEELS**

1979

DIRECTOR: Joan Micklin Silver.

SCREENPLAY: Joan Micklin Silver, from the novel by Ann Beattie.

CAST: John Heard, Mary Beth Hurt, Peter Riegert, Gloria Grahame, Kenneth McMillan.

Color, PG rated, 97m.

The cast is perfect in this charming comedy-drama about a government bureaucrat who becomes obsessed with an unhappily married woman. John Heard is especially likable as the misguided civil servant who falls head over heels for the woman who can't decide who, or what, she wants. Both Heard and Peter Riegert, as his unemployed jacket salesman friend, possess a talent for low-key comedy that makes this quiet gem sparkle.

CRIMES OF PASSION

1984

DIRECTOR: Ken Russell.

SCREENPLAY: Barry Sandler.

CAST: Kathleen Turner, Anthony Perkins, John Laughlin, Annie Potts.

Color, R rated (there is also an unrated version with added footage), 104m.

Generally considered pointless disgusting trash, we see *Crimes of Passion* as a hilarious satire on American sexual obsessions. Kathleen Turner revels in her role as a fashion designer who spends her nights as a hooker named China Blue, and Anthony Perkins delivers a demented parody of the psycho-killer cliché. Woven through the soundtrack is an unforgettably overwrought rendition of Dvorák's *New World Symphony.* All involved seem to be having a splendid time.

CROSSING DELANCEY

1988

DIRECTOR: Joan Micklin Silver.

SCREENPLAY: Susan Sandler, based on her play.

CAST: Amy Irving, Peter Riegert, Jeroen Krabbé, Reizl Bozyk, Sylvia Miles, Suzzy Roche.

Color, PG rated, 97m.

Amy Irving is marvelous as an independent young woman who moves out of her Lower East Side neighborhood to Greenwich Village, only to be pulled back when her meddling, well-intentioned grandmother, Bubbie (Bozyk), consults the neighborhood matchmaker to find Irving a husband. Already smitten with a self-absorbed writer (Krabbé), she isn't immediately impressed when introduced to pickle vendor Riegert, but his charm slowly starts to win her over. Terrific performances by Irving, Bozyk, and Riegert are the heart of this disarming romantic comedy.

DEFENDING YOUR LIFE

1991

DIRECTOR: Albert Brooks.

SCREENPLAY: Albert Brooks.

CAST: Albert Brooks, Meryl Streep, Rip Torn, Lee Grant, Buck Henry.

Color, PG rated, 111m.

Brooks is killed when his BMW hits a bus and he finds himself in Judgment City, where you can eat whatever you want, as much as you want, and never gain weight. With the help of advocate Rip Torn, he must defend his slothful, self-centered life if he is to move on to a higher level. He falls in love with fellow traveler Streep, who's so perfect that she'll undoubtedly move up, and Brooks is desperate to go with her. This intelligent examination of life and what may follow is the fourth of Brooks's underappreciated comedies. Brooks's real name is Albert Einstein. His brother, Bob Einstein, is better known as Super Dave.

THE DISORDERLY ORDERLY

1964

DIRECTOR: Frank Tashlin.

SCREENPLAY: Frank Tashlin.

CAST: Jerry Lewis, Glenda Farrell, Everett Sloane, Susan Oliver, Jack E. Leonard.

Color, Not rated, 90m.

Jerry runs wild in a convalescent home in this wacky story packed with slapstick. He plays Jerome Littlefield, a doctor wannabe who has to drop out of medical school because he suffers extreme sympathy pains. Full of zany highlights and a memorable ambulance chase finale, this movie is a good example of why Lewis has such a huge international reputation.

DOCTOR IN THE HOUSE

1954

DIRECTOR: Ralph Thomas.

SCREENPLAY: Nicholas Phipps, Richard Gordon, from stories by Richard Gordon.

CAST: Dirk Bogarde, Muriel Pavlow, Kenneth More, Donald Sinden, Kay Kendall, James Robertson Justice.

Color, Not rated, 92m.

Bogarde is Simon Sparrow, a first-year medical student at St. Swithin's Hospital. He soon finds that most of his fellow students are primarily interested in drinking, womanizing, and studying as little as possible to get by. This farce is full of sight gags and good-natured jabs at the medical profession. There's a memorable scene with a skeleton on a bus. First in a series of seven.

DOWN BY LAW

1986

DIRECTOR:	Jim Jarmusch.
SCREENPLAY:	Jim Jarmusch.
CAST:	Tom Waits, John Lurie, Roberto Benigni, Ellen Barkin, Billie Neal, Rockets Redglare.

B&W, R rated, 107m.

Waits and Lurie are down and out in New Orleans, languishing in jail until the lively Benigni is locked in with them and hatches a plan for escape. From then on the pace picks up as they hit the road and eventually wind up in a bar in the Louisiana swamp. Robby Müller's moody black and white photography is just right for this unconventional, but rewarding comedy. Waits and Lurie also provide the soundtrack music.

THE EFFICIENCY EXPERT

1992

DIRECTOR:	Mark Joffe.
SCREENPLAY:	Max Dann, Andrew Knight.
CAST:	Anthony Hopkins, Alwyn Kurts, Rebecca Rigg, Russell Crowe, Bruno Lawrence, Ben Mendelsohn.

Color, PG rated, 85m.

Hopkins's life is orderly, dull, and practical, so naturally he makes an ideal efficiency expert. On one fateful day he's summoned to Ball's moccasin factory, where he's confronted with a blissfully chaotic workplace full of cooperative, friendly people. Hopkins is faced with the dilemma of how to improve productivity without ruining the warm family atmosphere of the business. An easygoing comedy-drama with engaging characters and a lively score by Ricky Fataar.

THE FAMILY GAME

1983

DIRECTOR:	Yoshimitsu Morita.
SCREENPLAY:	Yoshimitsu Morita.
CAST:	Yusaku Matsuda, Juzo Itami, Ichirota Miyagawa, Junichi Tsujita.

Color, Not rated, 107m. Subtitled.

This delightful satire takes aim at the modern Japanese middle-class family, which, not surprisingly, has a lot in common with its Western counterparts. An intolerant and short-tempered tutor is hired to improve the youngest son's lackluster test scores so he can advance to a more prestigious school. Hilarity follows as the tutor takes it upon himself to straighten out every other member of the family as well. This uproarious movie was a box-office hit in Japan.

THE FUNERAL

1984

DIRECTOR:	Juzo Itami.
SCREENPLAY:	Juzo Itami.
CAST:	Nobuko Miyamoto, Tsutomu Yamazaki, Kin Sugai.

Color, Not rated, 124m. Subtitled.

The patriarch of a Japanese family dies and his daughter and son-in-law must engineer a traditional Buddhist funeral with all the trimmings. The actor son-in-law, saddled with the job of chief mourner, consults the video *The ABCs of Funerals* to learn his role. This singular black comedy lampoons Japanese funeral customs from soup to nuts, or should we say, from wake to cremation. This was the first film for Juzo Itami, who is best known in the U.S. for his "ramen western" comedy *Tampopo*.

FUNNYBONES

1995

DIRECTOR: Peter Chelsom.

SCREENPLAY: Peter Chelsom, Peter Flannery.

CAST: Oliver Platt, Lee Evans, Richard Griffiths, Leslie Caron, Jerry Lewis, Oliver Reed, Ian McNeice, George Carl, Freddie Davies, Ruta Lee.

Color, R rated, 126m.

Oliver Platt is a young comedian struggling to emerge from the shadow of his famous father (Lewis). After bombing in Las Vegas with his father in the audience, he returns to his birthplace in the English resort town of Blackpool to restart his career. Lee Evans is brilliant as the funniest and most peculiar of the old-time vaudevillians he meets there. This highly original and appealing story is filled with wonderful performances, including a very understated Lewis. Great score by John Altman.

THE GHOST BREAKERS

1940

DIRECTOR: George Marshall.

SCREENPLAY: Paul Dickey, Walter de Leon.

CAST: Bob Hope, Paulette Goddard, Paul Lukas, Willie Best, Richard Carlson, Lloyd Corrigan, Anthony Quinn.

B&W, Not rated, 85m.

After the success of *The Cat and the Canary* in 1939, Hope and Goddard team up once again in this light horror-comedy. Hope goes on the lam after witnessing a murder and ends up on the small Caribbean island where Goddard has just inherited a castle complete with ghosts, zombies, and buried treasure. Hope manages to keep the jokes coming no matter what the situation, and the hysterics are enhanced by an effectively spooky atmosphere. This movie has been imitated but never surpassed. Remade by Martin and Lewis as *Scared Stiff* in 1953.

THE GREAT MCGINTY

1940

DIRECTOR: Preston Sturges.

SCREENPLAY: Preston Sturges.

CAST: Brian Donlevy, Akim Tamiroff, Muriel Angelus, Louis Jean Heydt, Arthur Hoyt.

B&W, Not rated, 83m.

This witty political satire stars Donlevy as a hobo who gets hooked up with a crooked politician and rises in the political world from alderman to mayor, and finally to governor. First-time director Sturges won an Oscar for his superlative screenplay, and Donlevy and Tamiroff top a sterling ensemble cast.

THE HAIRDRESSER'S HUSBAND

1992

DIRECTOR: Patrice Leconte.

SCREENPLAY: Patrice Leconte.

CAST: Jean Rochefort, Anna Galiena, Roland Bertin, Maurice Chevit, Philippe Clevenot.

Color, Not rated (sexual situations), 84m. Subtitled.

After receiving a haircut at the age of 12, a man develops a lifelong obsession with voluptuous hairdressers, demonstrating how the seemingly minor experiences in life can leave the deepest impressions. A wistful erotic comedy with a somewhat dark underside. Flamboyant score by Michael Nyman.

THE HAPPIEST DAYS OF YOUR LIFE

1950

DIRECTOR: Frank Launder.

SCREENPLAY: Frank Launder, John Dighton, from the play by John Dighton.

CAST: Alastair Sim, Margaret Rutherford, Joyce Grenfell, John Turnbull, Guy Middleton.

B&W, Not rated, 83m.

Headmaster Sim is appalled to learn that due to clerical error, his beloved Nutbourne Academy for Boys has been invaded by headmistress Rutherford and a hundred girls from St. Swithin's. On top of the mayhem caused by the girls' arrival, the already frazzled staff tries to keep the calamity a secret from outsiders, especially parents. Their attempts at damage control prove futile as the frenzy reaches epic proportions. Sim and Rutherford are perfect foils in this brilliant farce.

HIGH HOPES

1988

DIRECTOR: Mike Leigh.

SCREENPLAY: Mike Leigh.

CAST: Philip Davis, Ruth Sheen, Edna Dore, Philip Jackson, Heather Tobias.

Color, Not rated (strong language), 112m.

Cyril and Shirley are a working-class, left-leaning couple just trying to get by in Thatcher's England. Cyril's sister is trying to live a middle-class life in the suburbs but seems desperately unhappy despite her manic cheerfulness. Mother, who's having trouble with her memory, lives in a rent-controlled flat next door to a couple of insensitive twits. Funny and touching, this bittersweet comedy is filled with memorable characters dealing with life's ups and downs.

THE HORSE'S MOUTH

1958

DIRECTOR: Ronald Neame.

SCREENPLAY: Alec Guinness, from the novel by Joyce Cary.

CAST: Alec Guinness, Kay Walsh, Renée Houston, Michael Gough, Ernest Thesiger.

Color, Not rated, 93m.

Guinness is wonderfully carefree as the gravel-voiced Gulley Jimson, an artist who manages to create his masterpieces while at the same time destroying everything around him. He squanders his money and is obliged to be a con man from time to time. He's never to be believed, relied upon, or trusted. Guinness's amazing performance didn't get him an Oscar nomination, but his screenplay did. The rousing score, based on Prokofiev's *Lieutenant Kije,* is perfect.

THE HOSPITAL

1971

DIRECTOR: Arthur Hiller.

SCREENPLAY: Paddy Chayefsky.

CAST: George C. Scott, Diana Rigg, Barnard Hughes, Nancy Marchand.

Color, PG rated, 102m.

Set in a large inner-city hospital, this searing black comedy could go a long way toward reducing skyrocketing medical costs. After watching it, most people would do anything to avoid getting sick. George C. Scott got an Oscar nomination for his portrayal of the suicidal head doctor forced to deal with political infighting, overwork, frightful incompetence (including a doctor who is hooked up to an IV by a nurse who didn't notice he was dead), and even murder. Chayefsky won an Oscar for his original screenplay.

HOT MILLIONS

1968

DIRECTOR: Eric Till.

SCREENPLAY: Ira Wallach, Peter Ustinov.

CAST: Peter Ustinov, Maggie Smith, Karl Malden, Bob Newhart, Robert Morley.

Color, G rated, 100m.

Peter Ustinov is a charmer as an ex-con embezzler who hatches a scheme to steal money from his corporate employer by programming the computer to write out huge checks to his phony companies. The supporting cast is also first-rate, with Maggie Smith as his seemingly naive girlfriend and Bob Newhart as a suspicious co-worker. The delightful screenplay, co-written by Ustinov and Ira Wallach, was nominated for an Oscar.

THE HOT ROCK

1972

DIRECTOR: Peter Yates.

SCREENPLAY: William Goldman, from the novel by Donald E. Westlake.

CAST: Robert Redford, George Segal, Zero Mostel, Paul Sand, Ron Leibman.

Color, PG rated, 105m.

This caper movie features a precisely done jewel heist, planned in each detail that gets bungled in every possible way. Robert Redford is the ringleader of a band of thieves who should have been comedians instead. Leibman is the maniacal getaway driver, Segal is the nerved-up lockpicker, and Sand is the bomb expert. A well-done crime story cleverly played for laughs.

HUSBANDS AND WIVES

1992

DIRECTOR: Woody Allen.

SCREENPLAY: Woody Allen.

CAST: Woody Allen, Judy Davis, Mia Farrow, Blythe Danner, Juliette Lewis, Liam Neeson, Sydney Pollack.

Color, R rated, 107m.

Pollack and Davis announce to their incredulous best friends (Farrow and Allen) that they're separating. What follows is a sometimes hysterical, sometimes uncomfortable exploration into the murky waters of adult relationships. This on-target look at marriage was unfairly maligned at the time of its release because of the publicity concerning Allen and Farrow's real-life problems. But Allen is one of the few Americans exploring this dangerous territory, and he's still the best at exposing his own and everyone else's insecurities and frailties with humor. Davis and Pollack are both standouts in an excellent cast.

IF I HAD A MILLION

1932

DIRECTOR: Ernst Lubitsch, Norman Taurog, Stephen Roberts, Norman Z. McLeod, James Cruze, William A. Seiter, H. Bruce Humberstone.

SCREENPLAY: Claude Binyon, Joseph L. Mankiewicz, Ernst Lubitsch, and others.

CAST: Gary Cooper, George Raft, Mary Boland, Charles Laughton, W. C. Fields, Wynne Gibson, Gene Raymond, Charlie Ruggles, Alison Skipworth, Jack Oakie, Frances Dee, Richard Bennett.

B&W, Not rated, 83m.

Wealthy Richard Bennett selects names from the phonebook and gives each a million dollars to see what they'll do. Each

episode in this all-star anthology has its own comedic style, but Charles Laughton, who quits his job with imagination, and W. C. Fields, who goes after road hogs with a vengeance, steal the show. Lighthearted fun.

I'M ALL RIGHT, JACK

1959

DIRECTOR: John Boulting.

SCREENPLAY: Frank Harvey, John Boulting, from the novel *Private Life* by Alan Hackney.

CAST: Ian Carmichael, Peter Sellers, Terry-Thomas, Irene Handl, Richard Attenborough, Dennis Price, Margaret Rutherford.

B&W, Not rated, 104m.

Stanley Windrush (Carmichael), dimwitted Oxford graduate, goes to work at his uncle's factory. His disastrous decision to start at the bottom inadvertently upsets the fragile peace between the union and the company, leading to a general strike. This scathing satire skewers both labor and management and is droll from beginning to end. Peter Sellers is a marvel as the beleaguered union boss who has to scramble to keep things running smoothly. Corruption and stupidity are in abundance, and everyone comes off looking very foolish indeed.

THE IN-LAWS

1979

DIRECTOR: Arthur Hiller.

SCREENPLAY: Andrew Bergman.

CAST: Peter Falk, Alan Arkin, Richard Libertini, Nancy Dussault.

Color, PG rated, 103m.

In this spy-comedy, Peter Falk, who claims to be with the CIA, ropes his future in-law Arkin, a conservative dentist, into his increasingly bizarre escapades. Arkin's facial expressions are priceless as Falk drags him from one dire situation to the next. Both actors are in top form. Libertini is excellent in a small part as a Latin American dictator with a peerless black-velvet art collection.

THE KING OF COMEDY

1983

DIRECTOR: Martin Scorsese.

SCREENPLAY: Paul D. Zimmerman.

CAST: Robert De Niro, Jerry Lewis, Sandra Bernhard, Diahnne Abbott, Tony Randall.

Color, PG rated, 109m.

Fruitcake Rupert Pupkin (De Niro) fancies himself a comedian, and he's so out of it he thinks kidnapping powerful talk-show host Jerry Langford (Lewis) in order to get a spot on his show is a good idea. Bernhard is the equally loony celebrity hound who helps Rupert, hoping to have a romantic interlude with her love object, Langford. De Niro's Rupert is someone you will not soon forget and will never want to meet. Lewis is convincing as the victim of his nefarious scheme. A disquieting look at the dark side of fame.

THE LADYKILLERS

1955

DIRECTOR: Alexander Mackendrick.

SCREENPLAY: William Rose.

CAST: Alec Guinness, Katie Johnson, Peter Sellers, Cecil Parker, Herbert Lom, Danny Green, Frankie Howerd.

Color, Not rated, 90m.

Sinister Alec Guinness, wearing big teeth, rents a room from lovely old landlady Johnson. There, he and his gang hatch plans for a robbery while attempting to keep the old woman in the dark. After the heist, they decide they'll have to bump her off, but their plans go awry, and one by one, each of them

is dispatched with great creativity. Katie Johnson won a British Academy Award as the sweet old lady, Mrs. Wilberforce. One of the best of the classic Ealing Studio comedies.

THE LAST DETAIL

1973

DIRECTOR: Hal Ashby.

SCREENPLAY: Robert Towne, from the novel by Darryl Ponicsan.

CAST: Jack Nicholson, Otis Young, Randy Quaid, Clifton James, Carol Kane, Michael Moriarty, Nancy Allen.

Color, R rated, 105m.

Certainly one of the most profane movies ever made, this road picture stars Nicholson as "Bad Ass" Buddusky, a foul-mouthed career sailor who draws what seems to be an easy detail escorting callow young sailor Quaid from Virginia to prison in Portsmouth, New Hampshire. Nicholson and his partner Otis Young take pity on the pathetic kid who faces eight years hard time, and the trip soon turns into a grungy initiation into the world of booze and women. Nicholson, Quaid, and Robert Towne's screenplay were all nominated for Oscars.

THE LAVENDER HILL MOB

1951

DIRECTOR: Charles Crichton.

SCREENPLAY: T. E. B. Clarke.

CAST: Alec Guinness, Stanley Holloway, Sidney James, Alfie Bass, Marjorie Fielding, Edie Martin.

B&W, Not rated, 78m.

Milquetoast bank teller Guinness hatches a scheme to steal a load of gold from the bank of England. He knows exactly how to get the job done down to the last detail, but somehow things do manage to go deliciously wrong. The terrific cast includes Audrey Hepburn in a small part. Another standout from Ealing Studios that won Oscars for its story and screenplay, and Guinness picked up an acting nomination.

LIFE IS SWEET

1991

DIRECTOR:	Mike Leigh.
SCREENPLAY:	Mike Leigh.
CAST:	Alison Steadman, Jim Broadbent, Claire Skinner, Jane Horrocks, Stephen Rea.

Color, R rated, 102m.

You won't soon forget this affectionate comedy about a middle-aged working-class couple and their distinctively different twin daughters. Horrocks is touching as the squeaky-voiced, fragile bulemic Nicola. Dad is a chef who buys an old beat-up snack wagon so he can be his own boss, and Mom (played by director Leigh's wife, Alison Steadman) cheerfully tries to hold the family together as they're beset by one crisis after another. This is an appealing comedy-drama about likable people, and it leaves you wishing them well. The lovely, lilting waltz score is by Rachel Portman.

LOST IN AMERICA

1985

DIRECTOR:	Albert Brooks.
SCREENPLAY:	Albert Brooks, Monica Johnson.
CAST:	Albert Brooks, Julie Hagerty, Garry Marshall.

Color, R rated, 91m.

Fast-track yuppie Brooks gets the boot, so he and wife Hagerty drop out in their new Winnebago to find the real America, by way of Las Vegas. After she loses the "core" of

their nest egg in the casino as he sleeps, they're forced to revise their plan. Filled with classic bits of Brooks's trademark neurotic humor, it demonstrates why he is considered the best in the business by other comedians. As Johnny Carson was quoted as saying, "I can't wait to see what he does next."

THE LOVED ONE

1965

DIRECTOR: Tony Richardson.

SCREENPLAY: Terry Southern, Christopher Isherwood, from the novel by Evelyn Waugh.

CAST: Robert Morse, Rod Steiger, Jonathan Winters, Anjanette Comer, John Gielgud, Liberace, Dana Andrews, Milton Berle, James Coburn, Tab Hunter, Margaret Leighton, Roddy McDowell, Robert Morley, Lionel Stander, Ayllene Gibbons.

B&W, Not rated, 116m.

A not-too-faithful adaptation of Evelyn Waugh's novel stands on its own as a biting satire on American culture in general and the funeral industry in particular. Englishman Morse comes to Los Angeles to bury his uncle (Gielgud) and falls for a cosmetologist (aptly named Aimee Thanatogenos) who's employed at the very exclusive mortuary. A multitude of outrageous performances, including Liberace as a casket salesman and Jonathan Winters as an unscrupulous clergyman, is topped by Rod Steiger as the unforgettable Mr. Joyboy. Thirty years after its release, this treat remains wonderfully offensive.

MISS FIRECRACKER

1989

DIRECTOR: Thomas Schlamme.

SCREENPLAY: Beth Hanley, from her play.

CAST: Holly Hunter, Mary Steenburgen, Tim Robbins, Alfre Woodard, Scott Glenn, Veanne Cox, Ann Wedgeworth.

Color, PG rated, 102m.

Holly Hunter leads an excellent cast in this portrait of an oddball family in Yazoo City, Mississippi. Hunter hopes that by entering the local Miss Firecracker contest she'll be accepted as a more normal member of the community. Steenburgen and Robbins are fine as her kooky cousins. This is one of those amiable little comedies that leaves you smiling.

CHUCK BARRIS

The Four Feathers (1939), directed by Zoltan Korda.

The Coca Cola Kid (1985), directed by Dusan Makavejev.

Dodsworth (1936), directed by William Wyler.

Two for the Road (1967), directed by Stanley Donen.

And Now my Love (1975), directed by Claude Lelouch.

Mr. Hulot's Holiday (1953), directed by Jacques Tati.

Chuck Barris created many television programs, including *The Dating Game* and *The Gong Show.* He is the author of the memoir *The Game Show King* and lives in Saint Tropez.

MR. HULOT'S HOLIDAY

1953

DIRECTOR: Jacques Tati.

SCREENPLAY: Jacques Tati, Henri Marquet.

CAST: Jacques Tati, Nathalie Pascaud, Michèle Rolla, Valentine Camax.

B&W, Not rated, 86m.

Jacques Tati introduces his gentle alter ego, Mr. Hulot, in this charming French comedy about a trip to the seashore. Mr. Hulot has a way of distracting people unintentionally with his odd walk and peculiar mannerisms. Using little dialogue, Tati relies on sight gags and subtle sound effects to create his easy-going humor. A refreshing entertainment.

MODERN ROMANCE

1981

DIRECTOR: Albert Brooks.

SCREENPLAY: Albert Brooks.

CAST: Albert Brooks, Kathryn Harrold, Bruno Kirby, Jane Hallaren, James L. Brooks.

Color, R rated, 93m.

Obsessive film editor Brooks keeps breaking up and making up with his girlfriend (Harrold). When the relationship is going well, he's compelled to ruin it. He can't help himself. A brilliantly funny portrait of the obsessive-compulsive personality, sprinkled with trenchant comic bits about the movie business. In her profile of Brooks for *The New Yorker*, author Alison Rose writes, "Any number of comics makes fun of neurosis; Brooks takes it as a given—as the fabric of American life...."

THE NASTY GIRL

1990

DIRECTOR: Michael Verhoeven.

SCREENPLAY: Michael Verhoeven.

CAST: Lena Stolze, Hans-Reinhard Müller, Monika Baumgartner, Elisabeth Bertram.

Color, PG-13 rated, 94m. Subtitled.

A young German woman (Stolze) decides to write an essay about her hometown and its role during the Nazi era for a national contest. She quickly discovers that most of the townspeople don't want to talk to her about it, and the city denies her access to public records. After she sues the city, she and her family receive threats and even have bombs thrown through their windows. Director Verhoeven gives us a dazzling example of creative filmmaking with this highly original and witty film that was based on a true story. Nominated for an Oscar for Best Foreign Film.

A NEW LEAF

1971

DIRECTOR: Elaine May.

SCREENPLAY: Elaine May.

CAST: Walter Matthau, Elaine May, Jack Weston, George Rose, James Coco, William Redfield.

Color, G rated, 102m.

Matthau is gilt-edged as an aging, self-indulgent bachelor who squanders his sizable trust fund by living too high off the hog. With no skills, no prospects, and no character, he decides his only alternative is to find a rich wife to murder. Elaine May stars as his inelegant and unfortunate target. She also wrote and directed this eccentric comedy. Coco and Weston shine in supporting roles.

NOISES OFF!

1992

DIRECTOR: Peter Bogdanovich.

SCREENPLAY: Marty Kaplan, from the play by Michael Frayn.

CAST: Carol Burnett, Michael Caine, Denholm Elliott, Julie Hagerty, Marilu Henner, Mark Linn-Baker, Christopher Reeve, John Ritter, Nicollette Sheridan.

Color, PG-13 rated, 104m.

This very funny film version of a Tony Award-winning play is directed at a break-neck pace by Peter Bogdanovich. The British-style farce about an acting troupe that suffers countless pitfalls and personal disasters during rehearsals and out-of-town performances boasts a splendid cast of big-name stars, all having a great time. Mass confusion and hysterics rule the day. A roaring artistic comeback for Peter Bogdanovich.

PANDEMONIUM

1982

DIRECTOR: Alfred Sole.

SCREENPLAY: Richard Whitley, Jaime Klein.

CAST: Tom Smothers, Carol Kane, Miles Chapin, Debralee Scott, Candy Azzara, Marc McClure, Judge Reinhold, Paul Reubens.

Color, PG rated, 82m.

A fiend is on the loose, killing cheerleaders at It Had to Be U. In the tradition of *Airplane!*, this parody of slasher movies tosses jokes out by the bushel basket as Bambi's Cheerleading Camp is besieged by psycho-killers, escaped convicts and mad scientists. Tom Smothers is the displaced Canadian Mountie who's investigating the case, assisted by his multi-talented horse, Bob, and his surly assistant, Johnson (Paul Reubens). Dandy star cameos by Eve Arden, Donald O'Connor, and Tab Hunter.

THE PRESIDENT'S ANALYST

1967

DIRECTOR: Theodore J. Flicker.

SCREENPLAY: Theodore J. Flicker.

CAST: James Coburn, Godfrey Cambridge, Severn Darden, Joan Delaney, Pat Harrington, Eduard Franz, Will Geer.

Color, Not rated, 104m.

In this underrated comedy-thriller, a psychiatrist is pursued by a multitude of government agents after he quits his job as the President's "secret shrink." James Coburn has a field day as the hip, womanizing title character, flashing his toothy grin at every opportunity. Severn Darden as a Russian spy, and Godfrey Cambridge as a CIA operative are standouts in supporting roles. Brilliant political satire.

REAL LIFE

1979

DIRECTOR: Albert Brooks.

SCREENPLAY: Albert Brooks.

CAST: Albert Brooks, Charles Grodin, Frances Lee McCain.

Color, PG rated, 99m.

Albert Brooks's first feature film is a sly send-up of cinéma vérité. In this pseudo-documentary satire on the PBS series *An American Family,* Brooks plays a shallow, self-absorbed Hollywood type, as only he can, who attempts to film the everyday life of a Phoenix veterinarian, with disastrous results. Charles Grodin is hilariously pathetic as the veterinarian who tries to put the best face on his disintegrating family life. Probably best known for his acting role in *Broadcast News,* Albert Brooks's own films display a singularly wicked humor that deserves a much wider audience.

ROSALIE GOES SHOPPING

1989

DIRECTOR: Percy Adlon.

SCREENPLAY: Percy Adlon, Eleonore Adlon, Christopher Doherty.

CAST: Marianne Sägebrecht, Brad Davis, Judge Reinhold, William Harlander, Erika Blumberger, Patricia Zehentmayr.

Color, PG rated, 94m.

German director Adlon and his leading actress Sägebrecht have moved on from the Bagdad Cafe to Stuttgart, Arkansas (the rice capital of America). Sägebrecht plays the German-born wife of loopy cropduster Davis, who's obsessed with providing her house full of kids with everything they desire. In fact, she shops so much that she has to devise a scheme using credit cards and her computer to stay ahead of their creditors. A wry comedy, with a friendly poke at America's love affair with shopping.

THE RULING CLASS

1972

DIRECTOR: Peter Medak.

SCREENPLAY: Peter Barnes.

CAST: Peter O'Toole, Harry Andrews, Alastair Sim, Arthur Lowe, Coral Browne, Michael Bryant.

Color, PG rated, 154m.

In this sardonic send-up of the upper classes, Peter O'Toole is absolutely balmy as a British aristocrat who believes he's Jesus Christ. But Alastair Sim nearly steals the show as a loony clergyman, his best role in almost twenty years. Filled with crazy characters and wild plot twists, this is a wildly funny satire that must be seen to be believed.

S.O.B.

1981

DIRECTOR: Blake Edwards.

SCREENPLAY: Blake Edwards.

CAST: Julie Andrews, Richard Mulligan, Robert Preston, William Holden, Robert Vaughn, Robert Webber, Larry Hagman, Shelley Winters, Loretta Swit.

Color, R rated, 121m.

This wickedly cynical satire is Edwards's potshot at Hollywood for the treatment he receives when his film *Darling Lili* flopped in the early '70s. It stars Richard Mulligan as Edwards's alter ego, a director who becomes suicidal when his latest movie seems destined to be a flop. In a haze of booze and drugs, a scheme is hatched to save the film by reworking the family movie into a sex flick featuring the wholesome-imaged star, played by his real-life wife Andrews, appearing topless. This savagely funny comedy was Holden's last film.

SAY ANYTHING

1989

DIRECTOR: Cameron Crowe.

SCREENPLAY: Cameron Crowe.

CAST: John Cusack, Ione Skye, John Mahoney, Lili Taylor, Amy Brooks.

Color, PG-13 rated, 100m.

This superior teen comedy is a believable and endearing story about a regular guy, Cusack, who falls for the beautiful class brain, Skye, the summer after high school graduation. Cusack and Skye are both appealing, and Mahoney is persuasive as Skye's overprotective father. In supporting roles, Lili Taylor grabs your attention as Cusack's lovelorn friend, and Cusack's sister is played by his real-life sister Joan. Screenwriter and first-time director Crowe, who is best known for *Jerry Maguire,*does it just right.

SHIRLEY VALENTINE

1989

DIRECTOR: Lewis Gilbert.

SCREENPLAY: Willy Russell, from his play.

CAST: Pauline Collins, Tom Conti, Julia McKenzie, Alison Steadman, Joanna Lumley, Sylvia Sims, Bernard Hill.

Color, R rated, 108m.

Collins recreates her London and Broadway stage successes as a middle-aged, working-class London housewife who takes off on holiday to Greece, leaving her demanding grown children and stick-in-the-mud husband to fend for themselves. Collins's comic asides to the camera are priceless, and her disarming performance won her an Oscar nomination. Playwright/screenwriter Russell also wrote *Educating Rita.*

SHOOT THE PIANO PLAYER

1960

DIRECTOR: François Truffaut.

SCREENPLAY: Marcel Moussy, François Truffaut, from the novel *Down There* by David Goodis.

CAST: Charles Aznavour, Nicole Berger, Marie Dubois, Michèle Mercier, Albert Rémy.

B&W, Not rated, 80m. Subtitled.

Here's a Truffaut masterpiece of a different sort. It's a daring combination of comedy and crime that finds downtrodden café pianist Aznavour suddenly mixed up with killers who mistake him for another gangster. It has a high-spirited, wide-open feeling due largely to the kinetic pacing and brilliant cinematography by Raoul Coutard. The story moves from cramped dark barrooms through city streets and culminates in a footchase across a mountain snowfield.

SLAP SHOT

1977

DIRECTOR: George Roy Hill.

SCREENPLAY: Nancy Dowd.

CAST: Paul Newman, Michael Ontkean, Lindsay Crouse, Jennifer Warren, Strother Martin, Melinda Dillon.

Color, R rated, 122m.

This wildly profane comedy about a losing small-town hockey team stars Paul Newman as its aging, womanizing coach. Unless their fortunes improve they'll all be out on the street, so Newman cynically takes on the ultraviolent and simple-minded Hansen brothers, and the fans can't get enough. This raunchy free-for-all is full of laughs and features a memorable striptease on ice by Michael Ontkean.

SMILE

1975

DIRECTOR: Michael Ritchie.

SCREENPLAY: Jerry Belson.

CAST: Bruce Dern, Barbara Feldon, Michael Kidd, Geoffrey Lewis, Nicholas Pryor, Colleen Camp, Annette O'Toole, Melanie Griffith.

Color, PG rated, 113m.

This acerbic satire takes aim at the best of Americana, the beauty pageant, and hits a bull's-eye. Solid citizen Bruce Dern is the harried organizer of a local pageant, faced with a blizzard of problems, including his son, who's selling candid Polaroids of naked contestants. Full of great moments, including some choice backstage scenes with Michael Kidd as an irascible, has-been choreographer attempting to whip the graceless young ladies into shape. A young Annette O'Toole is a dazzler as one of the contestants.

THE SNAPPER

1993

DIRECTOR: Stephen Frears.

SCREENPLAY: Roddy Doyle, from his novel.

CAST: Colm Meaney, Tina Kellegher, Ruth McCabe, Colm O'Byrne.

Color, R rated, 90m.

The turbulent life of an Irish working-class family is the subject of this touching comedy-drama. Colm Meaney (*Star Trek: The Next Generation*) is wonderful as the gruff but kindhearted father. Ruth McCabe is the sympathetic mother, and Tina Kellegher is the 20-year-old daughter who mortifies everyone by getting pregnant by the father of one of her friends. The charm of the film is in its disarming little bits of humor, such as the mailman singing "Return to Sender" as he delivers the mail, or the family singing "Tie a Yellow Ribbon" as the oldest son returns from the army.

STUART SAVES HIS FAMILY

1995

DIRECTOR: Harold Ramis.

SCREENPLAY: Al Franken.

CAST: Al Franken, Laura San Giacomo, Vincent D'Onofrio, Shirley Knight, Harris Yulin, Lesley Boone.

Color, PG-13 rated, 95m.

It's not bad enough that Stuart loses his *Daily Affirmations* program on public-access TV, but he's been summoned home to deal with a family crisis. Scary to think, but Stuart's the most emotionally stable member of his family. This film outing for Al Franken's *Saturday Night Live* self-help junkie, Stuart Smalley, is a sweet and surprisingly touching comedy-drama that was lost at the box office.

SUGARBABY

1984

DIRECTOR: Percy Adlon.

SCREENPLAY: Percy Adlon.

CAST: Marianne Sägebrecht, Eisi Gulp.

Color, Not rated (nudity, sexual situations), 87m. Subtitled.

This bittersweet story from West Germany features Marianne Sägebrecht as a lonely, overweight mortuary worker who plots to win the love of a married subway conductor. Sägebrecht's poignantly funny performance as the irrepressible woman makes this film special. She went on to star in *Bagdad Cafe* and *Rosalie Goes Shopping,* also directed by Percy Adlon, but has not been used effectively in the few American movies in which she's appeared. *Sugarbaby* displays her considerable talent well.

THE TALL BLOND MAN WITH ONE BLACK SHOE

1972

DIRECTOR: Yves Robert.

SCREENPLAY: Yves Robert, Francis Véber.

CAST: Pierre Richard, Bernard Blier, Jean Rochefort, Mireille Darc, Jean Carmet.

Color, PG rated, 90m. Subtitled.

Violinist Richard's life is turned upside down when a group of spies mistake him for a rival agent in this satisfying, easy to watch farce. Richard has a clumsy physical style of comedy all his own, and he uses it to great effect playing this ungainly and guileless character. The slam-bang finale features a madcap chase through the streets of Paris. Followed by *Return of the Tall Blond Man With One Black Shoe* (1974). Unsuccessfully remade with Tom Hanks as *The Man With One Red Shoe* (1985).

TATIE DANIELLE

1991

DIRECTOR: Etienne Chatiliez.

SCREENPLAY: Florence Quentin, Etienne Chatiliez.

CAST: Tsilla Chelton, Catherine Jacob, Isabelle Nanty, Neige Dolsky, Eric Prat.

Color, Not rated, 110m. Subtitled.

This French farce is about an unrepentent, crusty old lady who comes to live with her nephew and his family after her housekeeper has a mysterious accident. She proceeds to run roughshod over the lot of them until they hand her over to an equally cantankerous young woman who won't be pushed around. A fresh, unpredictable black comedy about a nightmare with gray hair.

A THOUSAND CLOWNS

1965

DIRECTOR: Fred Coe.

SCREENPLAY: Herb Gardner, from his play.

CAST: Jason Robards, Jr., Barbara Harris, Martin Balsam, Gene Saks, Barry Gordon.

B&W, Not rated, 118m.

Murray Burns was blissfully unemployed since quitting his job writing for a kids' TV show, raising his sister's 12-year-old son, Nick, in his own unconventional style. His ideal lifestyle comes to an end when child welfare decides to investigate his fitness to be his nephew's guardian. Harris is adorable as the social worker who falls for Robards and helps him turn reliable in time for the hearing. This witty comedy, adapted by Herb Gardner from his own successful play, was nominated for a Best Picture Oscar. Martin Balsam won a Supporting Actor Oscar as Robards's steady brother.

TIGHT LITTLE ISLAND aka WHISKEY GALORE

1948

DIRECTOR: Alexander Mackendrick.

SCREENPLAY: Compton Mackenzie, Angus Macphail, from the novel by Compton Mackenzie.

CAST: Basil Radford, Joan Greenwood, Jean Cadell, Gordon Jackson, James Robertson Justice, Wylie Watson.

B&W, Not rated, 82m.

This is a wonderful little Ealing Studios comedy about a ship full of whiskey wrecked off a small Hebridean island during World War II, and the lengths to which the islanders will go to commandeer its precious cargo. Gordon Jackson is superb as a young man who's delayed cutting the apron strings far too long. Topped off by a frantic chase scene.

USED CARS

1980

DIRECTOR: Robert Zemeckis.

SCREENPLAY: Robert Zemeckis, Bob Gale.

CAST: Kurt Russell, Gerrit Graham, Frank McRae, Jack Warden, Deborah Harmon.

Color, R rated, 112m.

Before *Back to the Future,* Robert Zemeckis and Bob Gale teamed up on this outrageously raunchy but good-natured lampoon of the used car business. The Fuchs brothers (both played by Jack Warden) run competing used car lots across the road from each other. When Luke Fuchs dies, head salesman Russell tries to conceal it from Luke's greedy brother, Roy, who'll inherit the lot. Bad taste is the rule here, and Russell is so astonishingly unscrupulous that you have to admire his style. This enterprising young man will do anything to sell a car, including hijacking the airways during a Presidential address to run a commercial. This is a rambunctious free-for-all with nonstop laughs.

KENNETH TURAN

The little-known talking pictures made by Warner Bros. in the early 1930s, just after sound came in and before the enforcement of the Production Code, cheerfully shattered taboos about sex, violence, and drug use. Raffish, exuberant and brash, they were made with an uncommon energy and frankness.

Baby Face (1933), directed by Alfred E. Green. Barbara Stanwyck starred in the most outrageous of the pre-Code movies, sold with the ad line, "She had IT and made IT pay."

Employee's Entrance (1933), directed by Roy Del Ruth. Warren Wellman, the king of pre-Code movies, gives an abrasive performance as a department store executive who lives up to his "smash or be smashed" motto.

Female (1933). Ruth Chatterton is a titan of industry who uses the handsome men in her company as sexual toys, dismissing them with bonuses when she gets bored.

Heroes for Sale (1933) and **Wild Boys of the Road*** (1933), directed by William Wellman. A pair of tough, gritty films with a surprising amount of social consciousness.

Kenneth Turan is the film critic for *The Los Angeles Times.* He lives in Pacific Palisades.

*This film is not yet available on video, but we can hope.

WHO AM I THIS TIME?

1982

DIRECTOR: Jonathan Demme.

SCREENPLAY: Morton Neal Miller, from the story by Kurt Vonnegut Jr.

CAST: Christopher Walken, Susan Sarandon, Robert Ridgely, Dorothy Patterson, Caitlin Hart, Les Podewell, Jerry Vile, Paula Francis.

Color, Not rated, 60m.

This enchanting short film features a wonderfully appealing performance by Christopher Walken as Harry Nash, the painfully shy hardware clerk who comes alive on stage in small-town community theater productions. Susan Sarandon is Helene Shaw, the new girl in town who falls hard for Harry when she plays Stella to his Stanley in *A Streetcar Named Desire*. The audition scene between Walken and Sarandon is a delight. This little charmer was originally shown on PBS's *American Playhouse*.

WITHOUT A CLUE

1988

DIRECTOR: Thom Eberhardt.

SCREENPLAY: Gary Murphy, Larry Strawther.

CAST: Michael Caine, Ben Kingsley, Jeffrey Jones, Lysette Anthony, Paul Freeman, Nigel Davenport.

Color, PG rated, 107m.

It turns out that Dr. Watson made the whole thing up. His fictional character Sherlock Holmes was so popular that he had to bring him to life with the help of a hired second-rate actor. That's the premise of this clever farce that, unfortunately, was largely ignored on first release. Ben Kingsley is excellent as Watson, the real brains of the duo who is forced to watch his oafish and most often drunk hireling,

Caine, take all the credit for his brilliance in solving cases. Caine is delightful as the easygoing and somewhat dimwitted Holmes impersonator, and his attempts at thinking on his own prove to be hilariously disastrous. An original and charming little comedy.

THE WRONG ARM OF THE LAW

1962

DIRECTOR: Cliff Owen.

SCREENPLAY: John Warren, Len Heath.

CAST: Peter Sellers, Lionel Jeffries, Bernard Cribbins, Davy Kaye, Nanette Newman, Bill Kerr, John Le Mesurier.

B&W, Not rated, 94m.

Sellers is Pearly Gates, a London crook who fronts as a wedding consultant with a very fake French accent. When a rival Australian gang starts stealing his mob's loot by impersonating the police, there's nothing to do but agree to a 24-hour no-crime truce to help the cops catch them. Sellers is right on the money in this slapstick cops-and-robbers farce, and Lionel Jeffries contributes his share of laughs as the bumbling Inspector Parker.

THE WRONG BOX

1966

DIRECTOR: Bryan Forbes.

SCREENPLAY: Larry Gelbart, Burt Shevelove.

CAST: John Mills, Ralph Richardson, Michael Caine, Peter Cook, Dudley Moore, Peter Sellers.

Color, Not rated, 105m.

An all-star cast propels this great-looking dark comedy set in Victorian England. Two elderly brothers (Mills and Richardson) are trying to kill each other over an inheritance.

Add to the mix Richardson's two greedy nephews (Cook and Moore) and Mills's grandson (Caine), and the stage is set for a case of who's got the body as corpses are dragged across the countryside in various assorted containers. Sellers is priceless as an eccentric doctor whose office is overrun by cats. With all this star power, Wilfrid Lawson steals the movie as the feeble, sarcastic butler Peacock.

Documentary

ACTING IN FILM: AN ACTOR'S TAKE ON MOVIE MAKING

Color, Not rated, 60m.

The craft of acting for the camera is the subject of this surprisingly entertaining and informative workshop given by Michael Caine for BBC television. Caine demonstrates how to talk to the camera, how to convey emotion, and most importantly, how to listen. He then runs the students through scenes and gives them tips to improve their performances. This fascinating look behind the scenes will be of interest not only to aspiring actors but to anyone who wants to get a better appreciation for what they're watching on screen in their favorite movies.

ALIVE: 20 YEARS LATER

1992

DIRECTOR: Jill Fullerton-Smith.

Color, Not rated, 51m.

This intriguing documentary revisits the survivors of a 1972 plane crash in the Andes Mountains. It was made during the production of the feature film *Alive,* which was based on their experiences. Of the 45 passengers and crew, 16 rugby players survived for 72 days on the flesh of their dead teammates. Some of the survivors visited the film set and found that although it brought back painful memories, it was helpful for them to talk about their experiences, some for the first time. These interviews offer a compelling record of what these young men endured. Narrated by Martin Sheen.

ANIMA MUNDI

1992

DIRECTOR: Godfrey Reggio.

Color, Not rated, 30m.

Following in the style of *Koyaanisqatsi* and *Powaqqatsi,* Reggio's third documentary in collaboration with composer Philip Glass is an exultation of the earth's natural beauty. This spellbinding combination of photography and music builds in intensity to the stunning finale featuring animals running, swimming, and in flight.

BEST BOY

1979

DIRECTOR: Ira Wohl.

Color, Not rated, 104m.

Wohl won an Academy Award for this filmed record of three crucial years in the life of his 52-year-old, mentally retarded cousin. Philly, who's been handicapped since birth, has always lived with his parents. After his father dies, his mother is unable to continue caring for him and he begins a journey to a more independent life, successfully making the transition into a group home before his mother dies. A highlight is Philly's backstage visit with Zero Mostel. This intimate record of daily life is both touching and filled with humor. Narrated by Wohl, it lovingly reveals the strength of the human spirit.

BROTHER'S KEEPER

1992

DIRECTOR: Joe Berlinger, Bruce Sinofsky.

Color, Not rated, 116m.

This amazing documentary details the unlikely case of Delbert Ward, one of four elderly brothers who shared a farm near Munnville, in upstate New York. They lived in what most would consider squalid conditions, which seemed to suit them fine. The only vehicle they owned was an old tractor. When brother William was found dead in the bed that he and Delbert shared, Delbert was arrested for his murder, though the evidence was far from compelling. As the trial approached, the small town rallied around the bewildered Delbert and made him an unlikely celebrity. The courtroom episodes are fascinating and take on an almost surreal quality as the prosecution tries to make its case. The power of this film is in the questions that it raises about our society's attitudes toward, and treatment of, people with little money or education.

BURDEN OF DREAMS

1982

DIRECTOR: Les Blank.

Color, Not rated, 94m.

Werner Herzog seems to have purposely decided to film his movie *Fitzcarraldo* under the worst conditions imaginable in the Peruvian jungles. Les Blank documents this obsessive, and some would say, insane, venture that Herzog wreaks on his crew and actors. In constant rain and knee-deep in mud, we watch in amazement the herculean effort undertaken to make *Fitzcarraldo,* a film which in the end turned out to be less compelling than this best-known of Blank's documentaries. Blank, who also made *Werner Herzog Eats His Shoe* (1980) about the director losing a bet with his then assistant, Errol Morris, was awarded the Maya Deren award for Outstanding Lifetime Achievement by an Independent Filmmaker by the American Film Institute in 1990.

CHUCK AMUCK: THE MOVIE

1989

DIRECTOR: John Needham.

Color, Not rated, 51m.

This is a lighthearted portrait of Chuck Jones, head animator at Warner Brothers during the glory days that made Bugs

Bunny, Daffy Duck, Porky Pig, Foghorn Leghorn, and Roadrunner household names. He demonstrates how he draws the characters and tells hilarious stories about the real people who inspired them. Jones has a natural, entertaining way of talking about his career, the results of which are the greatest series of cartoons in movie history, topped by the masterpiece *What's Opera, Doc?* A fascinating look at how cartoons are made.

CRUMB

1995

DIRECTOR: Terry Zwigoff.

Color, R rated, 119m.

This no-holds-barred look into the life of underground-comic artist Robert Crumb reveals practically everything there is to know, and probably more than should be known, about anybody. He's best known for his "Keep on truckin'" character, which brought him more attention than he wanted. Crumb reveals his uncensored innermost thoughts in his comics, which his readers may identify with, but would never want to admit. Much of the film examines Crumb's troubled family and childhood, including a look into the tragic lives of his brothers, Max and Charles.

GATES OF HEAVEN

1978

DIRECTOR: Errol Morris.

Color, Not rated, 85m.

This slightly daffy documentary about a beleaguered pet cemetery in Southern California may catch you off-guard. At first the cemetery workers and bereaved pet owners being interviewed seem completely off the wall. But you may be surprised by your own growing sympathy for these people as they reveal their heartfelt devotion to the furry departed. A classic slice of half-baked Americana.

HAROLD LLOYD: THE THIRD GENIUS

1989

DIRECTOR: Kevin Brownlow, David Gill.

B&W, Not rated, 120m.

Harold Lloyd is not a household name like Charlie Chaplin or Buster Keaton, but he was a hugely popular silent comedian in his own right, and he created some of the most spectacular comic stunts ever filmed. With his signature black-rimmed glasses and respectable suit, his character was an ordinary middle-class guy who found himself in the most perilous of predicaments. An athlete, Lloyd did many of his own complex and extended stunts, despite the fact that he'd lost his right thumb and forefinger in an explosion during the filming of *Haunted Spooks* in 1920. This entertaining portrait contains clips of some of his best work, as well as interviews with Lloyd and people who knew him.

I AM A DANCER

1973

DIRECTOR: Pierre Jourdan, Bryan Forbes.

Color, Not rated, 93m.

This film portrait of Rudolf Nureyev, one of the greatest male dancers of all time, is good enough to interest even those who aren't dance fans. Tracing his career from his early life in Russia to the world stage, it is filled with highlights of some of his greatest performances, in particular those with long-time partner Margot Fonteyn. But it is more the intimate scenes of his grueling practice schedule and the constant battles with a body in rebellion that offer an evocative look at what it takes to be the best.

KOYAANISQATSI

1983

DIRECTOR: Godfrey Reggio.

Color, Not rated, 90m.

Reggio is a former priest and social worker, so it's not surprising that all of his work concerns social and spiritual issues. The title is a Hopi Indian word meaning "crazy life, life in turmoil, life disintegrating, life out of balance, a state of life that calls for another way of living." Using aerial, slow-motion, and fast-motion photography, the camera glides across the American landscape, revealing an astonishing panorama of natural and manmade wonders. Set to a hypnotic score by Philip Glass, with no dialogue, this mesmerizing and gloriously beautiful film is a stunning sight and sound experience.

POLE TO POLE

1992

DIRECTOR: Roger Mills.

Color, Not rated, 400m.

British comedian and former Monty Python member Michael Palin is off on a trek from the north pole to the south pole, staying as close as possible to the 30th meridian by way of Finland, Russia, and East Africa. What makes it all so interesting are Palin's efforts to travel this straight line via any mode of transportation available, except airplane. Although he encounters all sorts of bizarre and unusual situations, the highlight of the trip is the friendliness and cooperation he gets from people along the way. This is a follow-up to Palin's attempt to follow the route taken by Jules Verne's hero, Phileas Fogg, around the world in 80 days.

POWAQQATSI

1988

DIRECTOR: Godfrey Reggio.

Color, Not rated, 99m.

Similar in style to his *Koyaanisqatsi,* Reggio again uses stunning photography and a powerful score by Philip Glass to expose the poverty and environmental destruction created in

the Third World by the developed countries. As in his previous film, he uses slow-motion and fast-motion photography with no narration to create an overwhelming cumulative impact.

SALESMAN

1968

Filmed by Albert and David Maysles.

B&W, Not rated (contains adult language), 90m.

This fascinating slice of life from the '60s follows four salesmen as they try to make a living selling Bibles door-to-door. Although it may not seem the most compelling subject for a documentary, it's an absorbing, tragic, and funny real-life drama. Focusing on Paul Brennan, an aging salesman who's having doubts about his ability to get the job done, it follows him as he goes into the homes of prospective buyers and delivers his pitch. But the most eye-opening moments are when the salesmen congregate in their motel room and talk about their life on the road. *Salesman* is a sympathetic portrait of some people you won't soon forget.

SHERMAN'S MARCH

1985

DIRECTOR: Ross McElwee.

Color, Not rated, 155m.

Ross McElwee starts out to make a film about General Sherman's march through the South during the Civil War. However, the affable McElwee gets sidetracked in a major way and winds up meandering from state to state looking up old girlfriends. A funny and touching odyssey of what could have been, and might still be, as he continues searching for love. McElwee's personal filmmaking style makes this special.

THE THIN BLUE LINE

1988

DIRECTOR: Errol Morris.

Color, Not rated, 106m.

This documentary has the feel of a Hollywood feature film, with a haunting soundtrack by Philip Glass. Loner Randall Adams was sentenced to death for the 1976 murder of Dallas policeman Robert Wood. Morris carried out a relentless and detailed investigation into the case, unearthing new evidence and interviewing witnesses. The result is a stunning indictment of a failed and abused justice system. The film was so persuasive that the case was reopened, Adams was freed, and the real killer was found to be in prison serving time for another murder. This is unforgettable filmmaking.

TIME INDEFINITE

1993

DIRECTOR: Ross McElwee.

Color, Not rated, 117m.

Ross McElwee follows up *Sherman's March* with this equally outstanding film centering on his family. His sense of humor is maintained as he reveals the joys and disappointments of those closest to him. McElwee plays a major role in his work, and his personality is what really drives these wonderful documentaries.

28 UP

1984

DIRECTOR: Michael Apted.

Color/B&W, Not rated, 136m.

British filmmaker Michael Apted (*Coal Miner's Daughter, Gorillas in the Mist*) filmed interviews with the same group of English schoolchildren at 7-year-intervals from age seven to twenty-eight. As they talk about their lives, dreams, and goals,

it's fascinating to see in what ways they change and grow over the years and yet how their basic personalities seem to have been set at an early age. Full of surprises, with some students doing well while others fall short of their promise. A fascinating and valuable record, followed by *35 Up*.

35 UP

1990

DIRECTOR: Michael Apted.

Color, Not rated, 127m.

A continuation in the series of interviews done at 7-year-intervals with the group of English children seen in *28 Up*, who are now well into adulthood. In many ways it's more interesting, but also more melancholy than the earlier film because resignation and loss of hope have set in for many of the interviewees. The series, which was produced for British television, is quite enlightening as a reflection of what it's like to be English. The series continues with *42 Up*.

W.C. FIELDS STRAIGHT UP

1986

DIRECTOR: Joe Adamson.

B&W, Color, Not rated, 100m.

This is a pure delight. Fields's son and many friends are interviewed for this loving tribute to one of the most distinctive movie comedians of all time. Loaded with clips from his greatest films, featuring the trademark wisecracks and sight gags that have become classics. Narrated by Dudley Moore.

Drama

ACCIDENT

1967

DIRECTOR: Joseph Losey.

SCREENPLAY: Harold Pinter, from the novel by Nicholas Mosley.

CAST: Dirk Bogarde, Stanley Baker, Jacqueline Sassard, Vivien Merchant, Michael York, Delphine Seyrig.

B&W, Not rated, 105m.

Spineless Oxford professor Bogarde lusts after his student Sassard in this portrait of sexual depravity and anguish. Stanley Baker is at his best as Bogarde's boorish rival. A centerpiece drunken dinner party reveals the characters at their boozy worst as they pick at each other's psyches. Director Losey, an American, was blacklisted in 1951 and moved to England. He was so productive there that he's often thought of as British. Losey and Pinter also worked together on *The Servant* (1963) and *The Go-Between* (1971). In the end Losey felt that his banishment was the best thing for his career. Michael York appears in his first major film role. Music by Johnny Dankworth.

AMERICAN HEART

1993

DIRECTOR: Martin Bell.

SCREENPLAY: Peter Silverman.

CAST: Jeff Bridges, Edward Furlong, Lucinda Jenney, Tracey Kapisky, Don Harvey.

Color, R rated, 113m.

This is a brutally honest film about an ex-con trying to start a new life. Jeff Bridges gives a daring performance as the well-intentioned loser who has a tenuous grip on a better future for himself and his 12-year-old son (Furlong). Living in a fleabag hotel in Seattle, dogged by his parole officer and scraping by taking any job he can find, he realizes that his past will be hard to shake. Bridges creates an unforgettable portrait of a man who keeps struggling, but doesn't even know what he needs to succeed. This is the first feature film for director Bell, who is best known for his Oscar-nominated documentary *Streetwise* (1985), also filmed in Seattle.

JOE AND VICTORIA KLEIN

JOE

Blume in Love (1973), directed by Paul Mazursky.

Thief (1981), directed by Michael Mann.

VICTORIA

The Mouse That Roared (1958), directed by Jack Arnold.

***The Greengage Summer** (1961), directed by Lewis Gilbert.

Accident (1967), directed by Joseph Losey.

Joe Klein writes a column for *Newsweek* and wrote the novel *Primary Colors*. **Victoria Klein** is a wife, mother, and homemaker. They live in Pelham, New York.

*This film is not yet available on video, but we can hope.

THE APPRENTICESHIP OF DUDDY KRAVITZ

1974

DIRECTOR: Ted Kotcheff.

SCREENPLAY: Mordecai Richler, from his novel.

CAST: Richard Dreyfuss, Micheline Lanctot, Randy Quaid, Jack Warden, Denholm Elliott.

Color, PG rated, 121m.

Dreyfuss is the ambitious young title character in this Mordecai Richler story set in 1948 Montreal. Duddy is a hustler who's always developing new schemes to make it rich. Denholm Elliott is hilarious in a supporting role as a has-been documentary filmmaker who's suckered in by Duddy to direct epic bar mitzvah and wedding films. Quaid plays an epileptic who's accidentally paralyzed as a result of Duddy's neglect. Dreyfuss gives an impressive performance as this manic dynamo in this early starring role. Winner of the Berlin Film Festival Golden Bear award.

AT CLOSE RANGE

1986

DIRECTOR: James Foley.

SCREENPLAY: Nicholas Kazan.

CAST: Sean Penn, Christopher Walken, Mary Stuart Masterson, Christopher Penn, Candy Clark, Crispin Glover.

Color, R rated, 115m.

Walken and Sean Penn are at their best in this chilling account of an incident that occurred in rural Pennsylvania in 1978. Delinquent brothers Sean and Christopher Penn decide it's cool to hang out with their estranged father Walken, a malevolent creep who's suddenly determined to take them under his wing. He's the head of a gang that's been pulling off robberies in the area, and the brothers decide to form their own gang to win his approval. What they don't realize, until it's too late, is that Walken's a callous killer. The threat of

violence hangs in the air, and Walken's menacing character is the stuff of nightmares. The Penns' real mother, Eileen Ryan, plays their grandmother.

THE BALLAD OF NARAYAMA

1983

DIRECTOR: Shohei Imamura.

SCREENPLAY: Shohei Imamura, from a novel by Shishiro Fukazawa.

CAST: Ken Ogata, Sumiko Sakamoto, Tonpei Hidari, Takejo Aki.

Color, Not rated (sexual situations, violence), 130m. Subtitled.

A legend tells of a primitive society a century ago in the mountains of northern Japan that manages to survive in the harsh environment only by killing off its elderly. At age 70, the eldest son must carry his parent up Mount Narayama to die alone of exposure. This stunningly photographed fable is framed around one old woman's impending one-way trip. The final scenes of the son struggling up the mountain with his mother on his back, overwhelmed with sadness and guilt, are extraordinary. This is a difficult, but rewarding film. Winner of the Palme D'Or at Cannes.

BILLY BUDD

1962

DIRECTOR: Peter Ustinov.

SCREENPLAY: Peter Ustinov, DeWitt Bodeen, from the novella by Herman Melville.

CAST: Robert Ryan, Peter Ustinov, Melvyn Douglas, Terence Stamp, David McCallum, Paul Rogers.

B&W, Not rated, 119m.

Ustinov produced, directed, co-wrote, and starred in this

handsome version of Melville's tale of good and evil, beautifully photographed by Robert Krasker. Billy Budd (Stamp) is an innocent young sailor conscripted from a merchant ship onto a British warship in 1797. Ryan is the sadistic master-at-arms who is compelled to destroy the purity of soul that's so apparent in Billy. Ustinov is the well-meaning captain who feels forced to choose justice over mercy. Stamp was nominated for a Best Supporting Actor Oscar. Inventive opening credits have the actors saying their character's name as their real name appears on the screen.

BLACK NARCISSUS

1946

DIRECTOR:	Michael Powell, Emeric Pressburger.
SCREENPLAY:	Michael Powell, Emeric Pressburger, from a novel by Rumer Godden.
CAST:	Deborah Kerr, David Farrar, Sabu, Jean Simmons.

Color, Not rated, 89m.

Deborah Kerr stars as the Sister Superior of a group of nuns who face physical and emotional adversity as they try to establish a mission in a remote area of the Himalayas. Considered the most spectacular color film ever made at the time of its release, it won an Academy Award for cinematographer Jack Cardiff. Though it takes place in the mountains, it was nearly all filmed on magnificent sets in the studio. Scenes of Kerr's past that were too shocking for American censors at the time of release have been restored. The final shots of the movie are among the most technically complex scenes ever filmed.

BLUE COLLAR

1978

DIRECTOR:	Paul Schrader.
SCREENPLAY:	Paul Schrader, Leonard Schrader.

CAST: Richard Pryor, Harvey Keitel, Yaphet Kotto.

Color, R rated, 114m.

His first time out as director, Paul Schrader offers a tough, gritty and profane look at life on an assembly line. Beaten down by management on one side and the union on the other, three cash-strapped auto workers hatch a plan to burglarize the union's safe. Pryor, Keitel, and Kotto all give gut-wrenching performances as these frustrated, embittered men with unsure futures.

BRIEF ENCOUNTER

1945

DIRECTOR: David Lean.

SCREENPLAY: Noel Coward, David Lean, Ronald Neame, Anthony Havelock-Allan, from the play *Still Life* by Noel Coward.

CAST: Celia Johnson, Trevor Howard, Stanley Holloway, Joyce Carey, Cyril Raymond.

B&W, Not rated, 86m.

This is a deeply touching masterpiece about an ill-fated, platonic love affair between two lonely, middle-aged people. Housewife Johnson and doctor, Howard meet by chance in a train station and share as much time as they can together over the next few days, agreeing at the end never to meet again. Brilliant photography combined with Rachmaninoff's stirring second piano concerto create an atmosphere impossible to forget. It can't be done any better. Academy Award nominations for Screenplay, Director, and Actress.

THE BROWNING VERSION

1951

DIRECTOR: Anthony Asquith.

SCREENPLAY: Terence Rattigan, from his play.

CAST: Michael Redgrave, Jean Kent, Nigel Patrick, Wilfrid Hyde White, Bill Travers, Ronald Howard.

B&W, Not rated, 90m.

Michael Redgrave gives an exceptionally well-drawn performance as a cheerless classics instructor at an English boys' school who's forced into retirement by illness. Hated by his wife (Jean Kent), who's having an affair with another teacher, he reevaluates his life and comes to the inescapable conclusion that he's a failure, until an act of kindness by a former student gives him the courage to face the future.

CARNY

1980

DIRECTOR: Robert Kaylor.

SCREENPLAY: Thomas Baum, from a story by Robbie Robertson, Robert Kaylor, Phoebe Kaylor.

CAST: Gary Busey, Jodie Foster, Robbie Robertson, Craig Wasson, Meg Foster, Bert Remsen, Kenneth McMillan.

Color, R rated, 106m.

This behind-the-scenes peek at the seedy world of the carnival business stars Busey and Robertson as hustlers who make their living off the easy marks who come to play. Busey makes your skin crawl with his dunk tank clown come-on routine. In a rasping voice reminiscent of Mercedes McCambridge's demon in *The Exorcist,* he suckers passersby into playing "Make Bozo Splash" by hurling insults at them. When Foster decides to escape from her boring small-town life and boyfriend Wasson, Busey takes her under his wing and convinces Robertson that they should allow her to join their exclusive society. A good evocation of the sinister atmosphere of carnival life. Score by Alex North.

THE CHOCOLATE WAR

1989

DIRECTOR: Keith Gordon.

SCREENPLAY: Keith Gordon, from the novel by Robert Cormier.

CAST: John Glover, Ilan Mitchell-Smith, Wally Ward, Jenny Wright, Bud Cort.

Color, R rated, 103m.

A middle-class Catholic prep school is the setting for this strong debut by writer-director Gordon. Brother Leon (Glover) relies on the assistance of the shadowy student group, the Vigils, to motivate students to double their quotas for the annual chocolate sale. When Jerry (Mitchell-Smith) defies both Brother Leon and the Vigils by refusing to sell chocolates, he faces reprisals from both. This is a powerful, cautionary tale about the lure of acceptance and the abuse of power.

CITY OF HOPE

1991

DIRECTOR: John Sayles.

SCREENPLAY: John Sayles.

CAST: Vincent Spano, Tony Lo Bianco, Joe Morton, Todd Graff, John Sayles.

Color, R rated, 129m.

The complexities of modern urban life are explored in this dizzying amalgam of stories about the intertwined lives of politicians, gangsters, police, workers, and street people in one neighborhood of a large Eastern city. Corruption, racial tensions, crime, and misplaced loyalties all have a devastating effect on these people's lives, and there seems to be no cure. Writer-director Sayles is one of the best at making entertainment with a social conscience, and he does it so consistently well.

CLOSE TO EDEN

1992

DIRECTOR: Nikita Mikhalkov.

SCREENPLAY: Nikita Mikhalkov, Roustam Ibraguimbekov.

CAST: Badema Bayaertu, Vladimir Gostukhin.

Color, Not rated (profanity, violence), 106m. Subtitled.

A Russian truck driver, falling asleep at the wheel, crashes in the middle of nowhere, which in this case is the Mongolian steppes just inside the Chinese border. He's given shelter by a Mongolian family and is soon won over by their warmth and infectious joy for life. Director Mikhalkov is known for his rapport with actors, and the performances here are uniformly delightful. The adorable little Mongolian boy is a natural charmer. These characters are all so well drawn, they seem like old friends. The Mongolian father's trip to town on horseback to buy a TV and condoms is hilarious. This stunningly photographed film will linger in your memory. Academy Award nomination for Best Foreign Language Film.

A CRY IN THE DARK

1988

DIRECTOR: Fred Schepisi.

SCREENPLAY: Robert Caswell, Fred Schepisi, from the book *Evil Angels* by John Bryson.

CAST: Meryl Streep, Sam Neill, Dale Reeves.

Color, PG-13 rated, 121m.

This real-life story of an Australian woman who was wrongfully convicted for the murder of her infant daughter is a parent's worst nightmare. No one believed the truth, that a dingo dog carried away her daughter while she and husband Neill were on a camping trip. The trial became the biggest story in Australia, creating a media circus that had her tried and convicted before she even stood trial. As the husband said, "Hell can't be worse than this." This skillfully directed

drama boasts superb performances from both Neill and Streep, who received an Oscar nomination.

DISTANT VOICES, STILL LIVES

1988

DIRECTOR: Terence Davies.

SCREENPLAY: Terence Davies.

CAST: Pete Postlethwaite, Freda Dowie, Angela Walsh, Dean Williams, Lorraine Ashbourne.

Color, PG-13 rated, 87m.

This lyrical work is an impressionistic collection of remembrances from British director Davies's working-class family life during and after World War II, set to the popular music of the era. Moments of terror with his mercurial, abusive father (Postlethwaite) are mixed with warm memories of his sister's marriage and wonderful nights singing at the pub. A highly personal and powerful film, followed by *The Long Day Closes.*

AN ENGLISHMAN ABROAD

1988

DIRECTOR: John Schlesinger.

SCREENPLAY: Alan Bennett.

CAST: Alan Bates, Coral Browne, Charles Gray.

Color, Not rated, 63m.

Coral Browne plays herself in this memoir about her meeting in the 1940s with exiled English spy Guy Burgess while she was performing Shakespeare in Moscow. She starts up a friendship of sorts after Burgess (Bates) bursts into her dressing room looking for cigarettes and liquor. After being invited to his dismal flat for tea, she agrees to buy some of the little things he misses most from England, including custom-made suits and shoes. Her visits to the exclusive shops in England that the socialist Burgess had frequented highlight the

irony of his situation. Bates gives an intriguing portrait of the lonely traitor. Made for British TV.

EUROPA, EUROPA

1991

DIRECTOR:	Agnieszka Holland.
SCREENPLAY:	Agnieszka Holland, from the autobiography of Solomon Perel.
CAST:	Marco Hofschneider, Rene Hofschneider, Julie Delpy, Ashley Wanninger, Piotr Kozlowski.

Color, R rated, 115m.

While fleeing the Nazis, a Jewish boy (Hofschneider) is mistakenly conscripted into the German army, where he becomes the mascot of his unit. After being taken under the wing by an officer, he's eventually sent to an elite Nazi youth school where he lives in constant terror of being exposed. Based on the autobiography of Solomon Perel, this is a miraculous story of courage and survival. Hofschneider is very appealing as the young Perel.

FAT CITY

1972

DIRECTOR:	John Huston.
SCREENPLAY:	Leonard Gardner, from his novel.
CAST:	Stacy Keach, Jeff Bridges, Susan Tyrrell, Candy Clark.

Color, PG rated, 96m.

It's hot in Stockton, California and everyone's sweating. Down-and-out boxer and fieldhand Keach works up a thirst and spends whatever hard-earned money he has boozing with Tyrrell, who plays a barfly so convincingly, you have to wonder if she's acting. He spots promising young boxer Bridges and helps promote him at funky small-time bouts.

This is certainly one of Keach's best performances, one of Huston's best films, and possibly the best movie ever made about boxing. The last scene sums up everything there is to know about these characters.

FEARLESS

1993

DIRECTOR: Peter Weir.

SCREENPLAY: Rafael Yglesias, from his novel.

CAST: Jeff Bridges, Isabella Rossellini, Rosie Perez, Tom Hulce, John Turturro.

Color, R rated, 122m.

Bridges is the lucky survivor of a horrendous plane crash. With only minor injuries, he helps rescue the injured and then walks calmly away from the scene. His life has changed in ways that he can't explain to his wife (Rossellini) and friends. He's not only lost his allergy to strawberries, he's lost his fear of death. This examination of the aftermath of tragedy builds to a shattering emotional climax, with a vivid slow-motion recreation of the plane crash. Stirring score by Maurice Jarre.

FLIRTING

1990

DIRECTOR: John Duigan.

SCREENPLAY: John Duigan.

CAST: Noah Taylor, Thandie Newton, Nicole Kidman.

Color, R rated, 99m.

In this sequel to *The Year My Voice Broke,* Taylor again plays Danny Embling, a smart but not popular student at an Australian prep school in the 1960s. After a dance at the girls' school across the lake, he becomes involved with Newton, the daughter of a Ugandan diplomat. Nicole Kidman is the stuck-up, blonde goddess who interferes in Newton's love life. This is a much better than average coming-of-age movie which takes a familiar theme and handles it extremely well.

GLENGARRY GLEN ROSS

1992

DIRECTOR: James Foley.

SCREENPLAY: David Mamet, from his play.

CAST: Al Pacino, Jack Lemmon, Ed Harris, Alan Arkin, Alec Baldwin, Kevin Spacey, Jonathan Pryce.

Color, R rated, 100m.

Mamet's savagely funny, profane look at the dog-eat-dog world of land development salesmen is bursting with great performances. The powerhouse cast revels in Mamet's dialogue, relieved perhaps that they're not actual inhabitants of this bleak world where, under extreme pressure to produce sales, humiliated and cajoled to compete with each other, they sometimes seem more like desperate caged animals than men.

A HANDFUL OF DUST

1988

DIRECTOR: Charles Sturridge.

SCREENPLAY: Charles Sturridge, Tim Sullivan, Derek Granger, from the novel by Evelyn Waugh.

CAST: James Wilby, Kristin Scott Thomas, Rupert Graves, Anjelica Huston, Judi Dench, Alec Guinness.

Color, PG rated, 118m.

Tony Last (Wilby) is a traditionalist who loves to stay at home on his ancestral estate with his son, but his wife (Kristin Scott Thomas) is bored and convinces him to let her take a flat in London. There she gets involved with an arrogant young opportunist. After their child dies and their marriage falls apart, Tony takes off on an expedition to Brazil. Wilby is

excellent as the unfortunate Mr. Last, and Alec Guinness has a small but choice role as an illiterate old madman. This is a well-done version of Evelyn Waugh's scathing satire on the privileged class in England, with lovely photography by Peter Hannan and score by George Fenton (*Jewel in the Crown*).

HEAVENLY CREATURES

1994

DIRECTOR: Peter Jackson.

SCREENPLAY: Frances Walsh, Peter Jackson.

CAST: Melanie Lynskey, Kate Winslet, Sarah Peirse, Diana Kent, Clive Merrison.

Color, R rated, 99m.

This true story of a sensational 1950s New Zealand murder case offers a stunning look into the twisted fantasy world of two teenage girls. Juliet Hulme was a flamboyant, attractive daughter of wealthy, educated parents. Pauline Parker was more quiet and introspective, from a working-class family. After meeting at school they became inseparable, and when their parents threatened to keep them apart, fearing that the relationship had become unnaturally close, the girls murdered Pauline's mother. The director, Peter Jackson, whose previous movies, *Bad Taste, Meet the Feebles,* and *Dead Alive,* have been in the gross-out horror genre, has done a masterful job of exploring the psychological aspects of this bizarre crime.

THE HEIRESS

1949

DIRECTOR: William Wyler.

SCREENPLAY: Ruth and Augustus Goetz, from their play suggested by *Washington Square* by Henry James.

CAST: Olivia de Havilland, Montgomery Clift, Ralph Richardson, Miriam Hopkins.

Color, Not rated, 115m.

Olivia de Havilland won an Oscar for her portrayal of the shy spinster daughter of a wealthy doctor in this screen version of Henry James's *Washington Square*. When the plain Catherine is courted by the handsome, penniless Morris Townsend (Clift), her father threatens to disinherit her if she marries him. Richardson's chilling performance as the rigid, pitiless father won an Oscar nomination, as did Wyler's confident direction. Aaron Copland provided the Oscar-winning score.

IN THE NAME OF THE FATHER

1993

DIRECTOR: Jim Sheridan.

SCREENPLAY: Terry George, Jim Sheridan, from the book *Proved Innocent* by Gerry Conlon.

CAST: Daniel Day-Lewis, Pete Postlethwaite, Emma Thompson, John Lynch, Corin Redgrave.

Color, R rated, 127m.

In this riveting, true-life drama, Day-Lewis plays Gerry Conlon, a troubled young man from Northern Ireland who was wrongly convicted of an IRA bombing in London in the 1970s. He, and three other innocent companions, spent 15 years in prison after being railroaded by the British legal system. His family in Ireland, convicted of aiding him, also did prison time. Pete Postlethwaite gives an unforgettable, heart-wrenching performance as Conlon's steadfast father, who goes to prison with his son, and dies there. Emma Thompson plays the lawyer who believes in their innocence and eventually wins them their freedom. This compelling drama from the team that made *My Left Foot* won Oscar nominations for Best Picture, Actor (Day-Lewis), Supporting Actor (Postlethwaite), Supporting Actress (Thompson), and Director. Title song by Bono.

JACKNIFE

1988

DIRECTOR: David Jones.

SCREENPLAY: Stephen Metcalfe, from his play *Strange Snow.*

CAST: Robert De Niro, Ed Harris, Kathy Baker, Charles Dutton, Loudon Wainwright III.

Color, R rated, 102m.

The arrival of Vietnam war buddy De Niro at the home Harris shares with his unmarried schoolteacher sister, Baker, is the catalyst that drives Harris to finally come to terms with his memories of the war and his guilt about the death of their high school friend. Truck driver De Niro and teacher Baker also start an unlikely romance. The characters ring true in this simple, heartfelt story about ordinary people trying to get by. Uniformly fine performances.

THE LAST BUTTERFLY

1991

DIRECTOR: Karel Kachyna.

SCREENPLAY: Ota Hofman, Karel Kachyna.

CAST: Tom Courtenay, Brigitte Fossey, Ingrid Held, Freddie Jones.

Color, PG-13 rated, 106m.

During the Nazi occupation of France, a famous Parisian mime (Courtenay) is coerced into entertaining the residents of Terezin (City of the Jews) to impress visiting Red Cross officials as to how well the inhabitants are being treated there. As Courtenay slowly becomes aware that this so-called model city is really just a midway point on the way to the gas chambers, he decides to put on a show that will convey the truth about the city and the Nazis' intentions to the Red Cross. Courtenay gives an accomplished performance in this haunting, melancholy tale.

THE LAST HOLIDAY

1950

DIRECTOR: Henry Cass.

SCREENPLAY: J. B. Priestley.

CAST: Alec Guinness, Beatrice Campbell, Kay Walsh, Bernard Lee, Wilfrid Hyde-White, Sidney James, Ernest Thesiger.

B&W, Not rated, 89m.

A surprisingly good-humored and charming story of a farm machinery salesman (Guinness) who's told by his doctor that he has a fatal illness. He decides to live out his time at a posh resort where he can do whatever he wants in a style that suits him. Supported by a willing cast of women who become infatuated with him and men who admire him, Guinness is brilliant as the amiable lead in this enchanting film. The superlative screenplay is by noted novelist and playwright J. B. Priestley.

LATE CHRYSANTHEMUMS

1954

DIRECTOR: Mikio Naruse.

SCREENPLAY: Sumie Tanaka, Toshiro Ide, from stories by Fumiko Hayashi.

CAST: Haruko Sugimura, Yuko Mochizuki, Chikako Hosokawa, Ken Uehara, Sadako Sawamura.

B&W, Not rated, 101m. Subtitled.

This quietly moving film follows the daily lives of four retired geishas as they eke out a living while trying to maintain their self-respect. Women are often at the center of Naruse's movies, and he makes a strong statement about the unequal status of women in Japanese society. He has a subtle, reflective style that creates an emotionally powerful effect. A moving tragicomedy, beautifully acted, from a director who deserves wider attention.

LET HIM HAVE IT

1991

DIRECTOR: Peter Medak.

SCREENPLAY: Neal Purvis, Robert Wade.

CAST: Christopher Eccleston, Paul Reynolds, Tom Bell, Eileen Atkins, Tom Courtenay, Michael Gough.

Color, R rated, 110m.

Yet another compelling true story of justice gone wrong, based on the 1952 case of a young man whose wrongful execution started the debate that ended the death penalty in England. A campaign started by his family won public sympathy but didn't save his life. Eccleston as Derek and Courtenay as his devoted father give convincing performances in this tough, disturbing film that director Medak doesn't allow to become maudlin.

LIGHT SLEEPER

1992

DIRECTOR: Paul Schrader.

SCREENPLAY: Paul Schrader.

CAST: Willem Dafoe, Susan Sarandon, Dana Delany, David Clennon, Mary Beth Hurt, Victor Garber.

Color, R rated, 103m.

Willem Dafoe is the restless title character, an aging delivery boy for an upscale New York drug dealer (Sarandon) whose attempt to renew a relationship with his addicted ex-girlfriend (Delany) ends in tragedy. It sounds grim, but it's suprisingly upbeat. Willem Dafoe is a highly versatile actor who once again proves his skill with this sincere and sympathetic performance. He and Sarandon have undeniable chemistry. With an excellent score by Michael Been.

THE LITTLE FOXES

1941

DIRECTOR: William Wyler.

SCREENPLAY: Lillian Hellman, from her play.

CAST: Bette Davis, Herbert Marshall, Teresa Wright, Richard Carlson, Charles Dingle, Dan Duryea, Carl Benton Reid, Patricia Collinge.

B&W, Unrated, 116m.

This is an outstanding screen adaptation of Lillian Hellman's play about the rapacious Hubbard family, set during the industrial rise of the South following the Civil War. Bette Davis heads a superb cast as the matriarch of this band of cutthroats who will stop at nothing to get their way. A Best Picture nomination, as well as nominations for writer Hellman, director Wyler, and actresses Davis and Wright were all well deserved.

LONELY HEARTS

1981

DIRECTOR: Paul Cox.

SCREENPLAY: Paul Cox, John Clarke.

CAST: Wendy Hughes, Norman Kaye, John Finlayson, Julia Blake, Jonathan Hardy.

Color, R rated, 95m.

An offbeat romantic comedy from Australia, this deceptively simple movie stars Wendy Hughes as a mousy, inexperienced office clerk who becomes involved with fifty-something piano tuner Kaye. Hughes and Kaye, who have both worked often with Dutch-born director Cox, are wonderful. Finlayson and Hardy are also delights as a flamboyant amateur theater director and as Peter's amiable, innocent brother-in-law. Kaye also provided the score.

THE LONELY PASSION OF JUDITH HEARNE

1987

DIRECTOR: Jack Clayton.

SCREENPLAY: Peter Nelson, from a novel by Brian Moore.

CAST: Maggie Smith, Bob Hoskins, Wendy Hiller, Marie Kean, Ian McNeice.

Color, R rated, 120m.

Smith is brilliant as Judith Hearne, a lonely middle-aged spinster who tries to give the impression that she's a well-to-do and respectable lady, but who in reality survives by giving piano lessons. After moving into a Dublin boarding house, she thinks she's found Mr. Right in the shape of the landlady's brother, ably played with an American accent by Bob Hoskins, who has recently returned from many years in the U.S. When the romance ends, she finds solace in drink. Remarkably, Moore was only 27 when he wrote this perceptive novel of middle-aged disillusionment. Ian McNeice also gives a sterling performance as the landlady's spoiled, overgrown twit of a son. Smith won the British Academy Award for her performance.

THE LONG DAY CLOSES

1993

DIRECTOR: Terence Davies.

SCREENPLAY: Terence Davies.

CAST: Marjorie Yates, Leigh McCormack, Anthony Watson, Nicholas Lamont, Ayse Owens.

Color, Not rated, 84m.

Davies's poetic and vivid autobiographical film is set in a working-class neighborhood in 1950s Liverpool. Eleven-year-old Bud (McCormack) has few friends other than his loving mother, and school is dull and dreary. He finds escape in the Hollywood musicals showing at the local movie theater, and the soundtrack is sprinkled with lines from classic films. But

it's the songs that his family shares together that offer the most uplifting and poignant moments. The movie has a dreamy quality, as if we were floating unseen in the room with the characters. Along with Davies's previous autobiographical film, *Distant Voices, Still Lives,* this is a truly unique and rewarding film. The closing moments, accompanied by a stirring rendition of the title song, are mesmerizing.

THE LONG VOYAGE HOME

1940

DIRECTOR: John Ford.

SCREENPLAY: Dudley Nichols, from four sea plays by Eugene O'Neill.

CAST: John Wayne, Thomas Mitchell, Ian Hunter, Ward Bond, Barry Fitzgerald, Wilfrid Lawson, Mildred Natwick, John Qualen.

B&W, Not rated, 104m.

One of the finest sea movies ever made, this superbly directed study of life aboard a merchant ship during World War II is distinguished by its cinematography and well-drawn characters. It features a strong ensemble cast with John Wayne as a hapless young seaman and a youthful Mildred Natwick in a small, but unforgettable scene with John Wayne in a café. Nominated for an Oscar for Best Picture, it also was nominated for its screenplay by Nichols, its score by Richard Hageman, and its brilliant cinematography by Gregg Toland, who was experimenting with many of the techniques he was to use so effectively in *Citizen Kane.* John Ford won an Oscar that year, but it was for his direction of *The Grapes of Wrath.*

MAD DOG AND GLORY

1993

DIRECTOR: John McNaughton.

SCREENPLAY: Richard Price.

CAST: Robert De Niro, Uma Thurman, Bill Murray, Kathy Baker, David Caruso, Mike Starr, Tom Towles, J. J. Johnston, Richard Belzer.

Color, R rated, 96m.

What an unfortunate title for this disarmingly sweet comedy-drama. De Niro stars as a shy, methodical police photographer whose ironic nickname is Mad Dog. Bill Murray also plays against type as a hard-boiled, world-weary gangster who offers girlfriend Glory (Thurman) to De Niro for a week as a reward for saving his life. De Niro and Thurman have an endearing chemistry, and De Niro's rendition of "That Old Black Magic" is memorable. Mike Starr is a standout in a supporting role as Bill Murray's polite henchman. The appearance by David Caruso as De Niro's police buddy was just before his successful stint on *NYPD Blue.*

THE MAGNIFICENT AMBERSONS

1942

DIRECTOR: Orson Welles.

SCREENPLAY: Orson Welles, from the novel by Booth Tarkington.

CAST: Tim Holt, Joseph Cotten, Dolores Costello, Anne Baxter, Agnes Moorehead, Ray Collins, Richard Bennett, Erskine Sanford.

B&W, Not rated, 88m.

This follow-up to *Citizen Kane* tells the story of the decline of a wealthy Midwestern family. Tim Holt is expert as the arrogant, swinish George Amberson Minafer, who, after running roughshod over everyone in his way, eventually gets his well-deserved come-uppance. The entire cast is grand, especially Cotten in a nuanced performance. Agnes Moorehead received an Oscar nomination for her complex portrayal of George's spinster aunt. Now an acknowledged

JOSH GREENFELD

***We Were Strangers** (1949). A John Huston picture about a pre-Castro Cuban revolutionary that is sometimes misguided and often doesn't make sense but is conceived with a rare passion and delivered with virtuoso performances by John Garfield, Jennifer Jones, Gilbert Roland, and Pedro Armendartz.

Salvador (1986). Remains Oliver Stone's best if least ballyhooed film. James Woods and James Belushi have never been better.

Catch-22 (1970). Just because Mike Nichols's film version isn't as good as Joseph Heller's original book doesn't mean it still isn't very funny. But unfortunately, when originally released, it was one of those films whose budget rather than laugh content and enjoyability quotient was reviewed.

The Magnificent Ambersons (1942). Orson Welles's version may have been shortened and recut by others, but it still remains a treatise in fine filmmaking. Middle America at the beginning of the 20th century has rarely been depicted as well, and it features a performance by the always underrated Joseph Cotten at the very top of his form.

The Bay Boy (1985). Daniel Petrie's sensitive coming-of-age story set in backwater Nova Scotia involving sexual awakening, murder, and a wayward priest is one of those small films, too easily overlooked during its theatrical release, that seems destined for a long video afterlife because its characters are so real they could just as easily be guests in your living room as visitors on a screen.

Josh Greenfeld received an Academy Award nomination for his screenplay *Harry and Tonto.* He lives in Pacific Palisades.

*This film is not available on video, but we can hope.

masterpiece, it was a box-office failure upon first release and resulted in RKO firing Welles and his troupe of actors. Stanley Cortez gave the film its distinctive look, and Welles delivers the effective narration. The score is by Bernard Herrmann.

MEAN STREETS

1973

DIRECTOR: Martin Scorsese.

SCREENPLAY: Martin Scorsese, Mardik Martin.

CAST: Harvey Keitel, Robert De Niro, David Proval, Amy Robinson, Richard Romanus.

Color, R rated, 112m.

Scorsese's first masterpiece was a critical, but not a box-office success. Keitel is Charlie, an ambitious small-time mobster who has to devote too much of his energy and money protecting his no-account, feckless pal, De Niro, from his creditors. De Niro gives a dynamic performance as the maniacal punk, Johnny Boy. Scorsese paints a tough, gritty portrait of life on the streets, where the grim threat of violence is always around the corner. Filmed in New York's Little Italy, the neighborhood where Scorsese grew up.

NAKED

1993

DIRECTOR: Mike Leigh.

SCREENPLAY: Mike Leigh.

CAST: David Thewlis, Lesley Sharp, Katrin Cartlidge, Greg Cruttwell.

Color, R rated, 126m.

Thewlis gives a savage performance as Johnny, a lost soul whose rage spills out onto everyone he meets. After raping a woman in Manchester, he shows up at his ex-girlfriend Louise's London apartment and proceeds to make himself at home. Between diatribes about the sorry state of the world

and being verbally abusive to her and her roommate, he also manages to be charming and manipulative when it suits him. He eventually pushes too far and ends up back on the street, where he preys on the sympathies of a night security guard to get out of the cold. For his devastating performance in this unflinching portrait of a man in pain, Thewlis was voted Best Actor by the New York Film Critics and at Cannes, and Leigh won best director at Cannes, but the film was ignored by Oscar. However, the more genteel *Remains of the Day* did receive several Oscar nominations that year.

THE NAKED CIVIL SERVANT

1975

DIRECTOR: Jack Gold.

SCREENPLAY: Philip Mackie.

CAST: John Hurt, Patricia Hodge, Liz Gebhardt, Stanley Lebor.

Color, Not rated (for adult audience), 80m.

This BBC production is based on the autobiography of well-known British homosexual Quentin Crisp. In the England of the 1930s and '40s, Crisp was an outrageous, flamboyant, and self-proclaimed effeminate homosexual. This funny and touching film shows the difficulties his lifestyle caused him during a time when homosexuality was illegal in England. Hurt won a British Academy Award for his engaging performance, which ranks in stature with his portrayal of Caligula in *I, Claudius*. As Crisp describes himself, "I am one of the stately homos of England."

NIGHT OF THE SHOOTING STARS

1981

DIRECTOR: Paolo Taviani, Vittorio Taviani.

SCREENPLAY: Paolo Taviani, Vittorio Taviani.

CAST: Omero Antonutti, Margarita Lozano, Massimo Bonetti, Norma Martelli.

Color, R rated, 106m.

The small Tuscan village of San Martino is threatened with destruction by the Nazis as the villagers wait for the American forces to liberate them in August 1944. This lyrical tale of a time of great sorrow and joy is told through the eyes of a six-year-old girl. Beautifully photographed, it's a haunting and personal portrait of life at a crucial moment in time. The Tuscan-born Taviani brothers were 13 and 15 respectively at the time of these events. The score is by Nicola Piovani.

NIGHT ON EARTH

1991

DIRECTOR: Jim Jarmusch.

SCREENPLAY: Jim Jarmusch.

CAST: Winona Ryder, Gena Rowlands, Giancarlo Esposito, Armin Mueller-Stahl, Rosie Perez, Isaach De Bankolé, Beatrice Dalle, Roberto Benigni, Paolo Bonacelli, Matti Pellonpaa.

Color, R rated, 125m.

On the same night, at the same exact time, people are in taxis in five different cities: Los Angeles, New York, Rome, Paris, and Helsinki. Like five short films we see each one as a separate slice of life. The drivers and fares all have stories to tell, with the standout probably being Benigni's hilarious monologue to a priest as he careens through the streets of Rome in typical Italian fashion, wearing sunglasses. Mueller-Stahl and Esposito are also good in the New York episode with Rosie Perez. A smart, original idea with an all-star cast.

OF MICE AND MEN

1992

DIRECTOR: Gary Sinise.

SCREENPLAY: Horton Foote, from the novel by John Steinbeck.

CAST: Gary Sinise, John Malkovich, Ray Walston, Casey Siemaszko, Sherilyn Fenn, John Terry.

Color, PG-13 rated, 110m.

Gary Sinise directed, co-produced and co-starred in this impressive version of the Steinbeck classic about wandering farmhands George (Sinise) and his dimwitted ward Lennie (Malkovich). Malkovich gives a powerful performance as the child-man Lennie, who is captivated by small animals and pretty girls but has a tendency to love things to death. This satisfying, but overlooked film is based on an outstanding screenplay by Horton Foote. Walston is excellent in a supporting role. Sinise and Malkovich were previously teamed up in the acclaimed production of Sam Shepard's *True West* (1983).

PATHS OF GLORY

1957

DIRECTOR: Stanley Kubrick.

SCREENPLAY: Stanley Kubrick, Calder Willingham, Jim Thompson, from the novel by Humphrey Cobb.

CAST: Kirk Douglas, Adolphe Menjou, George Macready, Wayne Morris, Richard Anderson, Ralph Meeker, Timothy Carey.

B&W, Not rated, 86m.

This overwhelming indictment of the insanity of war contains some of the most effective scenes of trench warfare ever filmed. During World War I, a French general orders an attack that fails miserably. Infuriated, he has three men chosen at random to be executed for cowardice as examples to the other soldiers. Kubrick lays out in detail the corruption and incompetence that permeated the military leadership. This film established Kubrick as a major director and has maintained its impact over the years. The cast gives powerful performances, with Douglas a standout as the officer assigned

to defend the three charged men. Banned in France upon release, it went largely unnoticed because of the popularity of another war movie, *The Bridge on the River Kwai,* which was released the same year.

PELLE THE CONQUEROR

1988

DIRECTOR: Bille August.

SCREENPLAY: Bille August, from the novel by Martin Nexo.

CAST: Max von Sydow, Pelle Hvenegaard.

Color, PG-13 rated, 138m. Available subtitled or dubbed.

At the turn of the century, Swedish widower von Sydow and his son Pelle (Hvenegaard) emigrate to Denmark in search of work. He's hired as a stable keeper at a large farm where they sleep in a cow barn. It's a harsh life. The winters are long, and the few joys they experience are savored. The acting is first rate (von Sydow was nominated for an Oscar), and the time and place are recreated in detail in this moving story about the lives of ordinary people. Winner of the Palme D'Or at Cannes, the Golden Globe and Oscar for Best Foreign Language Film.

PRETTY POISON

1968

DIRECTOR: Noel Black.

SCREENPLAY: Lorenzo Semple, Jr., from the novel *She Let Him Continue* by Stephen Geller.

CAST: Anthony Perkins, Tuesday Weld, Beverly Garland, John Randolph.

Color, Not rated, 89m.

Perkins and Weld are at their best in this bizarre drama about a quirky arsonist and the seductive high school pistol he recruits to assist him with his next project. Weld's hot for excitement and takes Perkins's flights of fancy to their lethal conclusion. Poor Perkins gets more than he bargained for in

this inventive little thriller. Filmed on location in Massachusetts.

PROOF

1991

DIRECTOR:	Jocelyn Moorhouse.
SCREENPLAY:	Jocelyn Moorhouse.
CAST:	Hugo Weaving, Genevieve Picot, Russell Crowe, Heather Mitchell.

Color, R rated, 91m.

Aloof and detached, blind photographer Weaving likes to have his photos described to him, but it has to be by someone he trusts. Blind since birth, he has nagging doubts that his mother may have lied to him as a child about what she saw. If she lied about that, how can he be sure that she loved him? His housekeeper (Picot) is in love with him, but is compelled to torment him by moving his furniture around because he doesn't return her feelings. An original, engrossing psychological drama with strong performances by Weaving, Picot, and Crowe as a restaurant worker who becomes involved in their cruel games. Great score by Not Drowning, Waving.

QUACKSER FORTUNE HAS A COUSIN IN THE BRONX

1970

DIRECTOR:	Waris Hussein.
SCREENPLAY:	Gabriel Walsh.
CAST:	Gene Wilder, Margot Kidder, Eileen Colgen, Seamus Ford.

Color, PG rated, 90m.

This refreshing story, filmed in Dublin, enters the life of Quackser Fortune (Wilder) as he faces some critical decisions. He enjoys his work collecting horse manure off the streets and

selling it to people for their gardens, but he knows that horse carts will soon be replaced by trucks. His family is pressuring him to get an education or go to America, but he knows that those aren't viable choices for him. It's about this time that he meets American student Kidder and gets involved in an unlikely relationship. He certainly doesn't fit in with her snooty university friends. Wilder gives a charming, understated performance as Quackser, and unlike many of his roles, he isn't the least bit frantic.

RACHEL, RACHEL

1968

DIRECTOR: Paul Newman.

SCREENPLAY: Stewart Stern, from the novel *A Jest of God* by Margaret Laurence.

CAST: Joanne Woodward, James Olson, Kate Harrington, Estelle Parsons, Donald Moffat, Terry Kiser.

Color, R rated, 101m.

Woodward received an Oscar nomination for her sensitive portrayal of a 35-year-old unmarried schoolteacher who's lived at home all her life with her grasping, small-minded mother. Her fantasies about sex and death are her only escapes from her desperately empty life until she has a brief affair with a stranger and gets pregnant. Now she must find the courage to start a new life. Newman does a commanding job in his first time out as director, and the film also received Oscar nominations for Best Picture, Screenplay, and Supporting Actress (Parsons).

RAISE THE RED LANTERN

1991

DIRECTOR: Zhang Yimou.

SCREENPLAY: Ni Zhen, from the novel *Wives and Concubines* by Su Tong.

CAST: Gong Li, Ma Jingwu, He Caifei, Cao Cuifeng, Jin Shuyuan.

Color, Not rated, 125m. Subtitled.

In a haunting performance, the remarkable Gong Li plays a young, university-educated woman who reluctantly becomes the fourth wife of a wealthy landowner in 1920s China. When she arrives, she finds that life here is a struggle of wills, as each of the women tries to undermine the others in order to have the coveted position of favorite wife. The film becomes a study of the intricate, ever changing relationships in the household, and Gong Li's fruitless attempts to find her place. Beautifully photographed, this sumptuous and brilliant film received an Oscar nomination for Best Foreign Film.

THE RETURN OF MARTIN GUERRE

1982

DIRECTOR: Daniel Vigne.

SCREENPLAY: Jean-Claude Carrière, Daniel Vigne.

CAST: Gerard Depardieu, Natalie Baye, Sylvie Meda, Maurice Barrier.

Color, Not rated, 111m. Subtitled.

Shortly after marrying, young Martin Guerre gets fed up with his life and disappears, leaving his new wife and strict father behind. He returns eight years later as a much more mature man. Is it the same person? Many of the villagers suspect that he's an imposter. Based on a true court case in 16th-century France, this film brilliantly evokes the look and feel of the time, and the ignorance of the people. A sensuous performance by Depardieu is the highlight of this romantic drama.

RUBY IN PARADISE

1993

DIRECTOR: Victor Nunez.

SCREENPLAY: Victor Nunez.

CAST: Ashley Judd, Todd Field, Bentley Mitchum, Allison Dean, Dorothy Lyman.

Color, R rated, 115m.

Ruby (Judd) leaves an unhappy past in rural Tennessee and takes off for the gulf coast of Florida to start a new life. Quiet, and determined to find her own way, she lands a job at a Panama City tourist shop run by Lyman. The performances are uniformly good, and Judd is a standout in her first film role. This unpretentious character study of a lovely young woman and the people she meets is directed in a gentle, relaxed style by Nunez. Charles Engstrom did the appropriately genial soundtrack.

SALAAM BOMBAY!

1988

DIRECTOR: Mira Nair.

SCREENPLAY: Sooni Taraporevala.

CAST: Shafiq Syed, Hansa Vithal, Chanda Sharma.

Color, Not rated (profanity), 114m. Subtitled.

Krishna is a 10-year-old boy, abandoned by his mother, who struggles to survive on the streets of Bombay while trying to raise the money to get home to his village. While in the city, he gets by on whatever job he can scrape up, delivering tea for a street vendor, committing petty crimes, and running errands for a prostitute. At one point he gets picked up by the police and spends some time in a reform school. A clear-eyed look at life on the street that is both horrifying and poetic. Syed gives a heartbreaking performance as the boy. This was Nair's directing debut.

SECRET HONOR

1984

DIRECTOR: Robert Altman.

SCREENPLAY: Donald Freed, Arnold M. Stone, from their play.

CAST: Philip Baker Hall.

Color, Not rated, 90m.

Richard Nixon spends an evening alone in his office, drinking heavily and reflecting back on his political life in this tour-de-force performance by Philip Baker Hall. Hall doesn't attempt an impersonation of Nixon like Anthony Hopkins in *Nixon.* Instead, he attempts to convey the essence of the man as he delivers a rambling monologue that reaches back to his early days in rural California and follows his entire political career, dwelling with particular venom on Henry Kissinger. Though this diatribe is dubious in its factual accuracy, it's funny, touching, and disturbing as it explores the wounds and grudges of a lifetime. In the end a surprisingly sympathetic look at the most fascinating figure in recent American politics.

SEVEN BEAUTIES

1975

DIRECTOR: Lina Wertmüller.

SCREENPLAY: Lina Wertmüller.

CAST: Giancarlo Giannini, Fernando Rey, Shirley Stoler, Elena Fiore.

Color, R rated, 115m.

Pasqualino (Giannini) is a gullible small-time gangster who fancies himself a ladies' man. He lives in Naples with his mother and seven fat sisters (the seven beauties). He's sent to an insane asylum after he kills a pimp, escapes, joins the Italian army and eventually ends up in a German concentration camp. Giannini's Pasqualino is a submissive worm who believes anything he's told by anyone who has

authority over him. In a memorable scene, he seduces the grotesque woman commandant of the camp. This brilliant, imaginative film is Wertmüller's crowning achievement. The film received Oscar nominations for Best Foreign Film, for Wertmüller as writer and director, and for Giannini as Best Actor.

SID AND NANCY

1986

DIRECTOR: Alex Cox.

SCREENPLAY: Alex Cox.

CAST: Gary Oldman, Chloe Webb, Drew Schofield, David Hayman.

Color, R rated, 111m.

This depiction of the downhill slide of '70s punk rocker Sid Vicious of the Sex Pistols and his American girlfriend, Nancy Spungen, is like watching a train wreck in slow motion; compelling, but hard to take at times. Their drug use and self-destructive behavior leave no doubt that they're on their way out. Oldman and Webb give mind-boggling performances as the doomed couple that leave you wondering how they prepared themselves on the set each day to get into character.

SIX DEGREES OF SEPARATION

1993

DIRECTOR: Fred Schepisi.

SCREENPLAY: John Guare, from his play.

CAST: Stockard Channing, Will Smith, Donald Sutherland, Ian McKellen, Mary Beth Hurt, Bruce Davison, Richard Masur, Anthony Michael Hall, Heather Graham, Eric Thal, Anthony Rapp.

Color, R rated, 111m.

A young black man charms his way into the home of a wealthy New York art dealer (Sutherland) and his wife (Channing), claiming that he's Sidney Poitier's son, and a classmate of their children at college. The couple realizes that they've been had after allowing him to stay the night, but what starts out as an amusing anecdote for the couple to share with dinner companions, eventually exposes the emptiness of their carefully constructed lives. The entire cast is superior in this fact-based film, but Stockard Channing is remarkable as a woman who is touched by this young imposter.

SOLDIER IN THE RAIN

1963

DIRECTOR:	Ralph Nelson.
SCREENPLAY:	Blake Edwards, Maurice Richlin, from the novel by William Goldman.
CAST:	Steve McQueen, Jackie Gleason, Tuesday Weld, Tony Bill, Tom Poston, Ed Nelson.

B&W, Not rated, 87m.

Army Supply Sergeant Gleason has the bearing of a general. With comical efficiency, he commands his little universe from behind his desk. McQueen is his admiring gofer and heir-apparent who gives unquestioning loyalty to his mentor. Based on the novel by William Goldman, this appealing comedy-drama offers ingratiating performances by Gleason and McQueen. Weld is good in a supporting role as a townie.

THE SUMMER HOUSE

1993

DIRECTOR:	Waris Hussein.
SCREENPLAY:	Martin Sherman, from the book *The Clothes in the Wardrobe* by Alice Thomas Ellis.
CAST:	Jeanne Moreau, Joan Plowright, Julie Walters, Lena Headey, David Threlfall.

Color, Not rated, 83m.

Jeanne Moreau steals the show in this production made for British television. She visits an old friend whose daughter has inexplicably agreed to marry the twit who lives next door with his mother (Plowright). After surveying the situation, Moreau takes it upon herself to get the wedding canceled, one way or another. Headey plays the betrothed young woman whose mysterious past in Egypt is revealed through breathtaking flashbacks. A captivating comedy-drama that succeeds because of the performances by Moreau and Plowright.

SUMMERTIME

1955

DIRECTOR: David Lean.

SCREENPLAY: H. E. Bates, from the play *The Time of the Cuckoo* by Arthur Laurents.

CAST: Katharine Hepburn, Rossano Brazzi, Isa Miranda, Darren McGavin.

Color, Not rated, 99m.

This beautifully photographed romance is a sure-fire inducement to visit Venice. Hepburn stars as an Ohio spinster on the vacation of a lifetime. She's come looking for adventure, and she soon finds it with a local shopkeeper (Brazzi), only discovering he's married after she's already fallen in love. Hepburn is radiant in a superb performance that won her an Oscar nomination. Lean was also nominated for his sensitive direction. The lovely cinematography by Jack Hildyard infuses the picture with a warm glow.

SUNRISE

1927

DIRECTOR: F. W. Murnau.

SCREENPLAY: Carl Meyer, adapted from *A Trip to Tibit* by Hermann Sudermann.

CAST:	Janet Gaynor, George O'Brien, Margaret Livingston.

B&W, Not rated, 97m.

A rural man and his wife take a trip to the city where the husband, seduced by another woman, is talked into murdering his wife. This deceptively simple silent film has a lyrical, sensual quality, and is considered by many to be at least one of the greatest films ever made. Filmed in Hollywood by German director Murnau, who came to the U.S. to take advantage of the filmmaking technology available here. Murnau was given complete control on the project, but when it didn't do well enough at the box office, Fox restricted his freedom in later movies. An Academy Award winner for Best Picture, it also won for its cinematography by Karl Struss and Charles Rosher, and lead actress Janet Gaynor.

THE SWEET SMELL OF SUCCESS

1957

DIRECTOR:	Alexander Mackendrick.
SCREENPLAY:	Clifford Odets, Ernest Lehman.
CAST:	Burt Lancaster, Tony Curtis, Susan Harrison, Marty Milner, Sam Levene.

B&W, Not rated, 96m.

Lancaster creates one of the most coldly monstrous characters on film as the all-powerful columnist J. J. Hunsecker, in this atmospheric tale of decadence and abuse of power. Favoritism is the name of the game, and he has no trouble enlisting the help of unscrupulous and ambitious press agent Curtis to break up his younger sister's romance with jazz musician Milner. The jazz score by Elmer Bernstein and nighttime photography by James Wong Howe help create a moody, sinister atmosphere. Brimming with razorsharp dialogue provided by Odets and Lehman. A fine supporting cast.

STEPHEN J. RIVELE

Andrei Rublev (1966), directed by Andrei Tarkovsky. The great Russian director's masterpiece, and the best sound film I have ever seen.

It's A Gift (1934), directed by Norman McLeod, with W. C. Fields. Fields's funniest film. The slow burn on the back porch is comic genius.

The Last Laugh (1924), directed by F. W. Murnau, with Emil Jannings. My favorite director's finest film and, I think, the best film ever made.

Five Easy Pieces (1970), directed by Bob Rafelson, with Jack Nicholson. A brilliant study in character and music.

Badlands (1974), directed by Terence Malick, with Martin Sheen. A powerful and dispassionate observation of the breathtaking banality of evil.

Stephen J. Rivele is the Oscar-nominated co-author of Oliver Stone's *Nixon* and author of the forthcoming novel *A Booke of Days.* He lives in Pasadena.

10 RILLINGTON PLACE

1970

DIRECTOR: Richard Fleischer.

SCREENPLAY: Clive Exton, from the book by Ludovic Kennedy.

CAST: Richard Attenborough, John Hurt, Judy Geeson, Pay Heywood, Andre Morell.

Color, PG rated, 111m.

Attenborough plays the notorious London serial killer John Christie in this true-crime story from the 1940s. Landlord Christie murdered the wife and child of his boarder Timothy Evans (Hurt) and framed him for the crimes. Evans was convicted and executed for the murders, and Christie continued to kill for many years before he was found out. Fleischer added an authentic flavor to this straightforward account of the case by filming it in the house and neighborhood where the crimes occurred.

THIS BOY'S LIFE

1993

DIRECTOR: Michael Caton-Jones.

SCREENPLAY: Robert Getchell, from the book by Tobias Wolff.

CAST: Robert De Niro, Ellen Barkin, Leonardo DiCaprio, Jonah Blechman.

Color, R rated, 115m.

DeCaprio plays Tobias Wolff in this autobiographical account of Wolff's troubled adolescence. DiCaprio moves to Seattle with his divorced mother (Barkin) to get a new start. Here she meets De Niro, who seems a nice enough guy with three children of his own. It's only after she marries him and they move to his small town in the Cascade Mountains, that he reveals his darker side. He reserves most of his venom for DiCaprio, who becomes a frequent target of his uncontrolled rage. The first rate acting in this searing drama is topped by DiCaprio's extraordinary performance.

THOUSAND PIECES OF GOLD

1991

DIRECTOR: Nancy Kelly.

SCREENPLAY: Anne Makepeace, from the novel by Ruthanne Lum McCunn.

CAST: Rosalind Choo, Chris Cooper, Dennis Dun.

Color, Not rated (profanity, suggested sex), 105m.

Set in the 1880s, this stirring independent film is based on the true story of a young woman (Choo) from northern China who is sold by her father and taken to San Francisco. From there she's sold to a Chinese saloonkeeper to be a prostitute in a mining town in Idaho. When she is saved from this fate by a well-meaning man who pays off her "owner," she struggles to earn the money to pay him back. This moving story of loss and perseverance is an engrossing look at the plight of Chinese immigrants during the gold rush years. Choo gives a memorable performance.

TOMORROW

1972

DIRECTOR: Joseph Anthony.

SCREENPLAY: Horton Foote, from his play based on a story by William Faulkner.

CAST: Robert Duvall, Olga Bellin, Sudie Bond, Richard McConnell, Peter Masterson.

B&W, PG rated, 103m.

A caretaker at a remote sawmill takes in an abandoned pregnant woman for the winter, and comes to love her. After marrying her on her deathbed, he takes her child back to his father's farm and raises him as his own, until her family shows up and takes the boy away. Duvall is totally convincing as the unassuming, illiterate man who stoically suffers the losses in his life. This simply told story of human endurance is considered the best filmed version of any of Faulkner's stories.

TRUE WEST

1983

DIRECTOR: Allan Goldstein.

SCREENPLAY: Sam Shepard, from his play.

CAST: Gary Sinise, John Malkovich.

Color, Not rated (profanity), 110m.

Sinise and Malkovich reprise their stage roles in this version of the Sam Shepard play shown on public television. Sinise also directed it for the stage. As it opens, hard-working screenwriter Sinise is housesitting for his mother, working on his latest script, when his manic and unpredictable brother Malkovich shows up unexpectedly. Malkovich has been living in the desert, burglarizing homes to survive. What follows is a nonstop, drunken free-for-all of destruction. Alternating between moments of hilarity and explosive anger, this unforgettable exploration of sibling rivalry run amok is what first brought Malkovich to public attention. He made his feature film debut in *The Killing Fields* in 1984.

TUNES OF GLORY

1960

DIRECTOR: Ronald Neame.

SCREENPLAY: James Kennaway, from his novel.

CAST: Alec Guinness, John Mills, Susannah York, Dennis Price, Kay Walsh, Duncan Macrae, Gordon Jackson.

Color, Not rated, 107m.

Mills and Guinness give sturdy performances in this character study of two peacetime military officers locked in a battle of wills. John Mills plays a young, disciplined colonel who takes over command of a Scottish regiment from Guinness, causing bitter resentment in the older man. The hard-drinking Guinness uses his popularity among his men to turn them against the competent but uncharismatic Mills, and the

conflict builds to a tragic conclusion. This riveting drama received an Oscar nomination for Screenplay. The surprisingly effective bagpipe score is by Malcolm Arnold. York appears in her film debut as Guinness's daughter.

TWELVE ANGRY MEN

1957

DIRECTOR: Sidney Lumet.

SCREENPLAY: Reginald Rose, from his play.

CAST: Henry Fonda, Lee J. Cobb, E. G. Marshall, Jack Warden, Ed Begley, Martin Balsam, John Fiedler, Jack Klugman.

B&W, Not rated, 95m.

Fonda leads a strong cast in this vehicle set in a jury room on a hot summer afternoon. Impatient to get done and go home, eleven men are ready to convict a young man for the murder of his elderly neighbor. Fonda isn't so sure, and he forces the others to reluctantly reexamine the evidence in detail. One by one the other jurors begin to have doubts in this taut and suspenseful study of group behavior. Lumet (*Dog Day Afternoon, Network*) received an Oscar nomination for this directing debut, which also received nominations for Best Picture and Best Screenplay.

TWICE IN A LIFETIME

1985

DIRECTOR: Bud Yorkin.

SCREENPLAY: Colin Welland.

CAST: Gene Hackman, Ann-Margret, Ellen Burstyn, Amy Madigan, Ally Sheedy, Brian Dennehy.

Color, R rated, 117m.

Hackman, a blue-collar worker whose home life has become routine, meets the new barmaid (Ann-Margret) at a neighborhood tavern and starts an affair. He eventually leaves

his bewildered wife (Burstyn) who is forced to reevaluate her own life as well. This sympathetic study of Hackman's midlife crisis and its effects on his family is elevated by its straightforward, unsensational viewpoint, and convincing performances by the leads. Madigan received an Oscar nomination for her role as the married daughter who can't accept her father's betrayal of her mother.

TWIST AND SHOUT

1984

DIRECTOR: Bille August.

SCREENPLAY: Bille August.

CAST: Adam Tonsberg, Lars Simonsen, Ulrikke Juul Bondo, Camilla Soeberg.

Color, Not rated (some nudity, sexual content), 99m. Available subtitled or dubbed.

This sweet, funny coming-of-age movie, set in Denmark, follows the friendship between a pair of teenage boys who play in a rock band together. One of the boys struggles with a difficult home situation while the other falls in love for the first time. The pain and joy of being a teenager ring true in this well-written, and acted, film. Bille August was trained as a still photographer, but started working as a cinematographer in the '70s. As a director he's best known for his 1987 Oscar-winning film *Pelle the Conqueror.*

UMBERTO D

1952

DIRECTOR: Vittorio De Sica.

SCREENPLAY: Cesare Zavattini, Vittorio De Sica.

CAST: Carlo Battista, Maria Pia Casilio, Lina Gennari.

B&W, Not rated, 89m. Subtitled.

In post-war Italy, a retired professor can barely survive on his meager pension, but he refuses to give up his mongrel dog, Flick. He and the dog wander the streets of Rome as he tries to find a solution to his dilemma. Filled with poignant moments and observations of everyday life, De Sica's heart-wrenching masterpiece is deceptively simple, yet overflowing with emotion, and builds to an unforgettable finale. De Sica has said this is his favorite movie. The original story by Zavattini received an Oscar nomination.

THE WATERDANCE

1992

DIRECTOR:	Neal Jimenez, Michael Steinberg.
SCREENPLAY:	Neal Jimenez.
CAST:	Eric Stoltz, Wesley Snipes, William Forsythe, Helen Hunt, Elizabeth Pena, Grace Zabriskie.

Color, R rated, 106m.

Stoltz stars as a writer who becomes a paraplegic after a hiking accident, in this fictional account of writer-director Jiminez's real-life experiences. He winds up in a rehabilitation center where he meets fellow paraplegics Snipes and Forsythe. Jiminez has created realistic, three-dimensional characters that are brought to life by the cast. This frank, unsentimental story conveys the joys and sorrows of the characters without becoming maudlin or overly emotional. The film compares favorably with *The Men,* starring Marlon Brando.

WHAT'S EATING GILBERT GRAPE?

1993

DIRECTOR: Lasse Hallström.

SCREENPLAY: Peter Hedges, from his novel.

CAST: Johnny Depp, Juliette Lewis, Mary Steenburgen, Leonardo DiCaprio, Crispin Glover.

Color, PG-13 rated, 117m.

It doesn't take long to figure out what's eating Gilbert (Depp). He lives in a small Iowa town with his morbidly obese mother, two sisters, and retarded brother (DiCaprio), working as a clerk at the local grocery store. His responsibility for DiCaprio's care can be overwhelming at times and his only outlet has been an obligatory affair with the local insurance agent's wife (Steenburgen). But his life takes a sudden upturn when Juliette Lewis shows up at a nearby campground on vacation with her grandmother. Depp and DiCaprio are both outstanding in this bittersweet and often funny film, and DiCaprio's remarkable performance won him an Oscar nomination as Best Supporting Actor. The talented cast includes Crispin Glover as the local undertaker.

THE WIND

1927

DIRECTOR: Victor Sjöström.

SCREENPLAY: Frances Marion, from the novel by Dorothy Scarborough.

CAST: Lillian Gish, Lars Hanson, Montagu Love, Dorothy Cummings.

B&W, Not rated, 75m.

Swedish director Sjöström came to America and made one of the finest movies of the silent era, starring Lillian Gish in her best performance. She plays a city girl who marries a gruff, uncouth farmer and moves with him to the dust bowl of

Texas. After killing a man who has raped her, she goes mad, and his ghost later haunts her during a howling dust storm. The photography and editing are so masterful you can almost feel the grittiness of the dust and the rattling and shaking of the house. Gish was considered the greatest actress of the silent era. This was her last major role.

WISE BLOOD

1979

DIRECTOR: John Huston.

SCREENPLAY: Benedict Fitzgerald, from the novel by Flannery O'Connor.

CAST: Brad Dourif, Daniel Shor, Amy Wright, Harry Dean Stanton, Ned Beatty, Mary Nell Santacroce.

Color, PG rated, 108m.

Army veteran Hazel Motes (Dourif) is determined to make a preacher of himself and starts sermonizing on street corners about his new "Church of the Truth Without Jesus." His first crusade is to debunk the itinerant evangelist Asa Hawks (Harry Dean Stanton), who claims to have blinded himself with quicklime to prove his faith in Jesus. Stanton is accompanied by his lustful daughter, Sabbath Lily (Wright), who develops an intense passion for Hazel that isn't returned. Dourif's Hazel Motes is a complex, disturbing character whose obsession to make himself "clean" ends in tragedy. This is a grim, but wonderfully strange movie that is often quite funny.

THE YEAR MY VOICE BROKE

1987

DIRECTOR: John Duigan.

SCREENPLAY: John Duigan.

CAST: Noah Taylor, Loene Carmen, Ben Mendelsohn, Graeme Blundell, Lynette Curran.

Color, PG-13 rated, 103m.

Writer-director Duigan gives us a satisfying coming-of-age story set in a small Australian town in the early 1960s. Fifteen-year-old Danny (Taylor) is a bright, likable teenage boy who works part-time in his father's bar. He develops a crush on Freya, a troubled girl with a dangerous boyfriend. Freya is an experienced and attractive girl, and Danny just likes being able to spend time with her, even if boyfriend Trevor is along. When the three of them get caught messing around an old run-down house, Danny's father decides to send him off to boarding school. The story of Danny's transition from childhood to adolescence begun here, is continued in *Flirting* (1990).

Family

ANDRE

1994

DIRECTOR: George Miller.

SCREENPLAY: Dana Baratta, from the book *A Seal Called Andre* by Harry Goodridge, Lew Dietz.

CAST: Keith Carradine, Tina Majorino, Chelsea Field, Aidan Pendleton, Shane Meier.

Color, PG rated, 94m.

A young Maine girl, Majorino, befriends a seal, and becomes the center of controversy in her small town in this fact-based story from the director of *The Man From Snowy River.* Her father (Carradine) supports her relationship with the seal when local fishermen and animal protection officials try to separate the two. Her older sister becomes jealous of the time and attention her father gives to her and the seal, and works with the fishermen against her. Majorino gives a winning performance as the determined girl. The lively soundtrack consists of early '60s pop music. In a controversial move, the coveted role of the East-Coast seal was snagged by a West-Coast sea lion.

BAKER'S HAWK

1976

DIRECTOR: Lyman D. Dayton.

SCREENPLAY: Dan Greer, Hal Harrison, from the novel by Jack Bickham.

CAST: Clint Walker, Burl Ives, Diane Baker, Lee H. Montgomery, Alan Young.

Color, G rated, 98m.

In this satisfying Western adventure, a young man (Montgomery) matures through his experiences helping his father (Walker) and the local sheriff subdue local vigilantes, who are threatening a recluse (Ives) the boy has befriended. A well-done coming-of-age story, beautifully filmed on location in Utah.

THE BRAVE ONE

1956

DIRECTOR: Irving Rapper.

SCREENPLAY: Harry Franklin, Merrill G. White, from a story by Dalton Trumbo.

CAST: Michel Ray, Rodolfo Hoyos, Elsa Cardenas, Joi Lansing, Carlos Navarro.

Color, Not rated, 100m.

A Mexican peasant boy's bull, Gitano, is sold and sent to the bullfighting ring in Mexico City, in this warm tale of a boy's love for his pet. He follows the bull to the city, and after finding him succeeds in rescuing him through sheer determination. The film won an Academy Award for its original story written by Dalton Trumbo. Trumbo was blacklisted in Hollywood at the time and used the pseudonym Robert Rich, causing major embarrassment to the Academy. Trumbo became the first blacklisted writer to use his real name, with the help of Kirk Douglas and Otto Preminger, who listed it in the credits for their films *Spartacus* and *Exodus*, both released in 1960.

THE CANTERVILLE GHOST

1944

DIRECTOR: Jules Dassin.

SCREENPLAY: Edwin Blum.

CAST: Charles Laughton, Margaret O'Brien, Robert Young, William Gargan, Rags Ragland, Peter Lawford.

B&W, Not rated, 95m.

Charles Laughton and Margaret O'Brien take turns stealing the show in this fantasy taken from a story by Oscar Wilde. Laughton is a 17th-century ghost who is doomed to haunt an English castle. It seems that Laughton was a coward in his former existence, and he won't be free until his descendent (Young) does an heroic deed. Laughton plays the unfortunate ghost in a typically flamboyant style.

FRANKENWEENIE

1984

DIRECTOR: Tim Burton.

SCREENPLAY: Lenny Ripps.

CAST: Shelley Duvall, Daniel Stern, Barret Oliver.

B&W, PG rated, 27m.

In a typical suburban neighborhood, young Victor Frankenstein's dog, Sparky, gets hit by a car. Victor (Barret) decides he can bring him back to life using various household appliances and his swing set, aided by a timely thunderstorm. The revived dog proceeds to terrorize the neighborhood, and a vigilante committee forms. Will Sparky survive? This early effort by Tim Burton (*Beetlejuice, Batman*) captures the mood and style of the original *Frankenstein* and adds a large dose of laughs. May be too scary for younger children.

THE GEISHA BOY

1958

DIRECTOR: Frank Tashlin.

SCREENPLAY: Frank Tashlin.

CAST: Jerry Lewis, Suzanne Pleshette, Marie McDonald, Sessue Hayakawa, Nobu McCarthy.

Color, Not rated, 98m.

Bumbling magician Lewis joins a USO tour to Japan with his furry partner Harry the Rabbit (in a brilliantly crafted performance by Harry Hare). In Japan he gets friendly with WAC Pleshette (in her screen debut) and a small orphaned boy who wants to go home with him. Filled with local color and loads of sight gags with Harry the Rabbit that kids will love. Sessue Hayakawa provides a big laugh as the little boy's grandfather who's building a very familiar looking bridge in his garden. The L.A. Dodgers appear in cameos.

GEORGE'S ISLAND

1991

DIRECTOR: Paul Donovan.

SCREENPLAY: Maura O'Connell, Paul Donovan.

CAST: Ian Bannen, Sheila McCarthy, Maury Chaykin, Nathaniel Moreau, Vicki Ridler, Brian Downcy, Gary Reineke.

Color, PG rated, 90m.

George (Moreau) is a Nova Scotian boy who's sent to a foster home instead of being allowed to live with his salty old grandfather (Bannen), whose gruesome tales about Captain Kidd and his hidden treasure have captured the 10-year-old's imagination. George escapes from the foster home and takes off in a stolen boat with his grandfather and a schoolmate to discover an island that's a boy's paradise. He's convinced that the island holds a buried treasure, guarded by pirate ghosts

as described in his grandfather's stories. Imaginative, rousing good fun, with a fanciful score by Marty Simon. There is some cartoonish violence that may be too intense for younger children.

THE GOLDEN AGE OF COMEDY

1957

DIRECTOR: Compiled by Robert Youngson.

B&W, Not rated, 78m.

This collection of sight gags from the silent comedies made at the Max Sennett and Hal Roach studios includes clips from the Keystone Cops, Harry Langdon, Will Rogers, Jean Harlow, Ben Turpin, Stan Laurel and Oliver Hardy, and more. It's been widely praised and may be without parallel. Pauline Kael described the Laurel and Hardy custard pie clip as "a demonstration that throwing a pie can be both art and science." Laurel and Hardy are featured often, and for good reason. Narration is included but isn't needed.

A GRAND DAY OUT

1989

DIRECTOR: Nick Park.

SCREENPLAY: Nick Park.

CAST: Peter Sallis (voice).

Color, Not rated, 25m.

Nick Park introduces his characters, Wallace and Gromit, in this clay-animation short subject. Wallace is a happy-go-lucky inventor who builds a rocket ship with the aid of his levelheaded and put-upon dog, Gromit. Together they take a trip to the moon to collect cheese. Winner of the British Academy Award and nominated for an Oscar for animated short subjects along with his *Creature Comforts*. Park was responsible for the award-winning animation in Peter Gabriel's music video *Sledgehammer.* Music by Julian Nott.

GREGORY'S GIRL

1980

DIRECTOR: Bill Forsyth.

SCREENPLAY: Bill Forsyth.

CAST: Gordon John Sinclair, Dee Hepburn, Jake D'Arcy, Claire Grogan.

Color, PG rated, 91m.

Gregory has suddenly grown too tall, and he's too clumsy to be of any use on the school soccer team. He falls in love with the newest and best member of the team, a girl named Dorothy. His infatuation is all he thinks about, except perhaps his band. A fresh approach to teenage love and the heartache and insecurity that accompanies it, this often hilarious and always good-natured comedy was filmed in Scotland. Winner of the British Academy Award for Best Screenplay.

INTO THE WEST

1992

DIRECTOR: Mike Newell.

SCREENPLAY: Jim Sheridan, David Keating.

CAST: Gabriel Byrne, Ellen Barkin, Ciarán Fitzgerald, Ruaidhri Conroy, David Kelly, Johnny Murphy, Colm Meaney.

Color, PG rated, 97m.

A thrilling story of two boys who save a magical white horse from a brutal man in Dublin and escape with it into the west of Ireland. The boys are members of the Travellers, the wandering descendents of an ancient Celtic tribe. Byrne, their father, goes searching for them. Their adventures will appeal to children and adults alike. The film has a lyrical and mysterious quality, and is filled with Irish references to the meaning and importance of family ties. Byrne was also an associate producer.

RANDY SUE COBURN

The Miracle (1991). I like it even better than Neil Jordan's next film, *The Crying Game.*

Local Hero (1983), directed by Bill Forsyth. An all-time favorite of mine that lots of people have missed.

Carmen (1983). Carlos Saura's version.

Choose Me (1984), directed by Alan Rudolph.

Ball of Fire (1941). Howard Hawks directing from a Billy Wilder script.

Sweetie (1990) and **An Angel at My Table** (1991), directed by Jane Campion.

Randy Sue Coburn, who co-wrote the film *Mrs. Parker and the Vicious Circle,* is a Seattle-based writer.

LEONARD MALTIN'S ANIMATION FAVORITES FROM THE FILM BOARD OF CANADA

1994

DIRECTOR: Sally Roy.

Color, Not rated, 95m.

The National Film Board of Canada has been producing wonderful animated short films for many years now, as well as other short subjects and documentaries. Many of them have won Academy Awards. The problem is that no one gets to see them, so this compilation is a valuable corrective. The shorts featured in this collection are all as special as their individual creators. There isn't any consistent style or theme. One of the best is "The Cat Came Back." Maltin discusses the shorts at the beginning of the tape.

MIGHTY JOE YOUNG

1949

DIRECTOR: Ernest B. Schoedsack.

SCREENPLAY: Ruth Rose.

CAST: Terry Moore, Ben Johnson, Robert Armstrong, Frank McHugh, Douglas Fowley.

B&W, Not rated, 94m.

This kinder, gentler variation on *King Kong* is about an oversized ape who's taken from Africa by the young woman who's raised him as a pet to appear in a Hollywood nightclub. Generally mild-mannered, he seems to have a particular dislike for lions, but can usually be pacified by hearing "Beautiful Dreamer," his favorite song. This exciting adventure, complete with happy ending, may be too intense for younger children. Academy Award winner for the special effects by Willis O'Brien and Ray Harryhausen, who also did *King Kong*. Director Schoedsack and star, Armstrong, are also reunited from *King Kong*.

MYSTERIOUS ISLAND

1961

DIRECTOR: Cy Endfield.

SCREENPLAY: John Prebble, Dan Ullman, Crane Wilbur, from the novel by Jules Verne.

CAST: Michael Craig, Herbert Lom, Gary Merrill, Joan Greenwood, Michael Callan.

Color, Not rated, 101m.

During the Civil War, Union soldiers escaping from a Confederate prison in a balloon drift out to sea, where they eventually land on an island. Threatened by giant animals, they're forced to seek shelter in a cave, where they encounter the infamous Captain Nemo and his *Nautilus,* which is now out of service. With Nemo's help, they work out a plan of

escape. This adventure yarn, a sequel, of sorts, to *20,000 Leagues Under the Sea,* has plenty of thrills, including some of Ray Harryhausen's best special effects. Enjoyable score by Bernard Herrmann.

OUR VINES HAVE TENDER GRAPES

1945

DIRECTOR: Roy Rowland.

SCREENPLAY: Dalton Trumbo, from the novel by George Victor Martin.

CAST: Edward G. Robinson, Margaret O'Brien, James Craig, Agnes Moorehead, Jackie "Butch" Jenkins.

B&W, Not rated, 105m.

This is a pleasant, old-fashioned movie about a year in the life of a Norwegian farm family in Wisconsin. In a surprising bit of casting, Robinson is wonderful as the calm, patient father. Agnes Moorehead is his wife, and O'Brien is his sweet, adorable daughter. The film concentrates on the events of everyday life, with crisp dialogue and amusing scenes and good performances.

THE OUTSIDE CHANCE OF MAXIMILIAN GLICK

1988

DIRECTOR: Allan A. Goldstein.

SCREENPLAY: Phil Savath.

CAST: Saul Rubinek, Jan Rubes, Noam Zylberman, Susan Douglas Rubes.

Color, G rated, 96m.

In this delightful coming-of-age film set in the 1960s, Max (Zylberman) is a precocious 12-year-old Jewish boy who lives with his family in a small Canadian town. He's preparing for his bar mitzvah with the local young rabbi (Rubinek) whose frankness and unconventional ways have caused a stir,

and his conservative Jewish family doesn't approve of his friendship with a young gentile girl with whom he wants to enter a piano competition. Zylberman is wonderful as the irrepressible and ambitious Max, who's eager to try all that life has to offer.

THE RAILWAY CHILDREN

1972

DIRECTOR: Lionel Jeffries.

SCREENPLAY: Lionel Jeffries, from the novel by E. Nesbit.

CAST: Dinah Sheridan, Bernard Cribbins, William Mervyn, Iain Cuthbertson, Jenny Agutter.

Color, G rated, 102m.

After their father is falsely imprisoned as a spy, three children and their mother are forced to leave their stately London home and move to a remote cottage in the Yorkshire countryside. The children love to watch the trains passing by on the nearby railway tracks, and they begin waving to the passengers aboard. To their delight, the passengers start waving back. A relationship begins between the children and one of the regular passengers, which has a profound effect on their family's future. Filled with wonderful characters and some exciting adventures, this lovely film, set in 1905, was the directing debut for well-known character and comic actor Lionel Jeffries.

RING OF BRIGHT WATER

1969

DIRECTOR: Jack Couffer.

SCREENPLAY: Jack Couffer, Bill Travers, from a book by Gavin Maxwell.

CAST: Bill Travers, Virginia McKenna, Peter Jeffrey, Roddy McMillan, Jameson Clark.

Color, G rated, 107m.

From the stars of *Born Free* comes this story about a writer (Travers) who moves to the western highlands in England and befriends an otter. It's beautifully photographed and filled with funny and touching moments, with the rascally otter stealing the show, of course. This endearing little film is an unexpected delight that hasn't been widely seen.

SAFETY LAST

1923

DIRECTOR: Sam Taylor, Fred Newmeyer.

SCREENPLAY: Harold Lloyd, Sam Taylor, Tim Whelan, Hal Roach.

CAST: Harold Lloyd, Mildred Davis, Noah Young.

B&W, Not rated, 70m.

Lloyd is an ambitious young man who leaves his small town to make it big in the city. To impress his girlfriend, he enters a contest to climb a skyscraper, and what follows is a spectacular series of stunts and sight gags that set the standard for others to emulate. Lloyd did more of the dangerous stunts than even he had planned after his stunt man broke his leg. This comedy classic can still deliver screams of delight.

THE SECRET OF ROAN INISH

1994

DIRECTOR: John Sayles.

SCREENPLAY: John Sayles, from the novella *The Secret of Ron Mor Skerry* by Rosalie Fry.

CAST: Jeni Courtney, Eileen Colgan, Mick Lally, Richard Sheridan, John Lynch.

Color, PG rated, 103m.

Fiona is a young Irish girl sent to live with her grandparents on the west coast of Ireland. Her grandfather (Lally) tells her stories of the Caneelly family and the mysterious creatures

called Selkies, half-human and half-seal, who live on their ancestral island of Roan Inish. This is a simple story, beautifully told. Mason Daring did the lovely score, and Haskell Wexler's cinematography is magical.

SO DEAR TO MY HEART

1949

DIRECTOR: Harold Schuster.

SCREENPLAY: John Tucker Battle, from the book *Midnight and Jeremiah* by Sterling North.

CAST: Burl Ives, Beulah Bondi, Bobby Driscoll, Luana Patten, Harry Carey.

Color, Not rated, 84m.

This lesser-known Disney plum tells the simple story of a small boy (Driscoll) and the mischievous black lamb he wants to enter in the county fair. Set in 1903, it's a loving, nostalgic look at rural life at its most idyllic, interspersed with colorful animated sequences. Burl Ives, as Uncle Hiram, sings "Lavender Blue," the Oscar-nominated song by Eliot Daniel and Larry Morey, and several other charming songs. Driscoll is a delight, and Beulah Bondi is wonderful as his long-suffering mother.

THE SUNDOWNERS

1960

DIRECTOR: Fred Zinnemann.

SCREENPLAY: Isobel Lennart, from the novel by Jon Cleary.

CAST: Robert Mitchum, Deborah Kerr, Peter Ustinov, Glynis Johns, Dina Merrill, Michael Anderson Jr., Wylie Watson.

Color, Not rated, 133m.

Mitchum is Paddy Carmody, an Australian sheep drover who travels from one job to the next with his loyal wife (Kerr)

and son (Anderson). He enjoys the lifestyle, but his wife and son would rather save their money for a down payment on a farm of their own. Mitchum takes on Ustinov, a former merchant seaman who's always ready with a sea yarn to tell, and who quickly becomes part of the family. This heartwarming story, set in the 1920s, was beautifully filmed on location by Jack Hildyard. Though it received Oscar nominations for Best Picture, Screenplay, Director, Actress (Kerr), and Supporting Actress (Johns), this epic never received the attention it deserved. Winning performances all around, with Ustinov providing the comic relief. Music by Dimitri Tiomkin.

THREE SMART GIRLS

1936

DIRECTOR: Henry Koster.

SCREENPLAY: Adele Commandini, Austin Parker.

CAST: Deanna Durbin, Barbara Read, Nan Grey, Charles Winninger, Binnie Barnes, Ray Milland, Alice Brady, Mischa Auer, Ernest Cossart, Hobart Cavanaugh, Nella Walker.

B&W, Not rated, 86m.

Deanna Durbin made her screen debut in this enchanting musicomedy about three lively daughters who try to bring their divorced parents back together. But first they have to rescue their father from the greedy clutches of fortune hunter Barnes and her mother (Brady). Mischa Auer provides the best comedy moments as a drunken count. Audiences were bewitched by Durbin's extraordinary singing voice and exuberant personality, and she became an overnight star. This box-office hit was also nominated for an Oscar as Best Picture. It's lost none of its appeal over the years, and its infectious, good-natured charm will leave you smiling.

A TREE GROWS IN BROOKLYN

1945

DIRECTOR: Elia Kazan.

SCREENPLAY: Tess Slesinger, Frank Davis, from the novel by Betty Smith.

CAST: Dorothy McGuire, Joan Blondell, James Dunn, Lloyd Nolan, Peggy Ann Garner.

B&W, Not rated, 128m.

This warmhearted reminiscence, set in the tenements of turn-of-the century Brooklyn, tells the story of a poor Irish family through the eyes of a young girl (Garner). Francie's father, a heavy-drinking charmer, is beloved by everyone, especially Francie. Francie dreams of becoming a writer, and her father helps her get enrolled in a better school. Her mother (McGuire), who has the thankless job of holding the family together, relies heavily on Francie for help. Filled with warmth and humor, this is an emotionally and artistically satisfying directing debut for Kazan. The cast is superb, with Blondell a standout as McGuire's loving sister.

WHEN COMEDY WAS KING

1960

DIRECTOR: Compiled by Robert Youngson.

B&W, Not rated, 81m.

This is Youngson's second great compilation of the best clips from the heyday of sight gags and comic thrills. The print quality is very good. The choicest material was selected from the best comedy classics of the silent era. Included are Laurel and Hardy, Buster Keaton, Keystone Cops, Charlie Chaplin, Gloria Swanson, Fatty Arbuckle, and others.

WHISTLE DOWN THE WIND

1961

DIRECTOR: Bryan Forbes.

SCREENPLAY: Keith Waterhouse, Willis Hall, from the novel by Mary Hayley Bell.

CAST: Hayley Mills, Bernard Lee, Alan Bates, Norman Bird, Elsie Wagstaff, Alan Barnes.

B&W, Not rated, 99m.

In the north country of England, three children find a murderer (Bates) hiding out in a barn, and believe that he's Jesus Christ fleeing his persecutors. Featuring authentic dialogue and great performances by Hayley Mills and six-year-old Alan Barnes, this beautifully done allegory may be the best movie ever made about how children interpret the world around them. This was Forbes's directing debut. The original story was written by Hayley's mother, Mary Hayley Bell.

THE WORLD OF HENRY ORIENT

1964

DIRECTOR: George Roy Hill.

SCREENPLAY: Nora Johnson, Nunnally Johnson, from a novel by Nora Johnson.

CAST: Tippy Walker, Merri Spaeth, Peter Sellers, Angela Lansbury, Paula Prentiss, Phyllis Thaxter, Tom Bosley.

Color, Not rated, 106m.

Two lonely 14-year-old girls develop a fantasy world around famous pianist Henry Orient (Sellers), complete with secret language. Sellers, who's having an affair with a married woman (Prentiss), becomes paranoid when he sees the girls following him around town. This poignantly funny story of adolescence is an overlooked pleasure. Good performances, especially by Lansbury as the distant, self-absorbed mother of one of the girls.

THE WRONG TROUSERS

1993

DIRECTOR: Nick Park.

SCREENPLAY: Nick Park, Bob Baker.

CAST: Peter Sallis (voice).

Color, Not rated, 30m.

Inventor Wallace and his downtrodden dog, Gromit, return after *A Grand Day Out* in this delightful clay-animation adventure. Wallace has invented a pair of robotic "techno-trousers" that allow their wearer to climb buildings and do other useful tricks. A little short of cash, Wallace takes in a mysterious lodger, a sinister-looking penguin whom Gromit distrusts immediately. Everyone will love this Oscar winner, animated by Nick Park and Steve Box. The lively score is by Julian Nott.

Fantasy/Sci-Fi

THE ADVENTURES OF BUCKAROO BANZAI ACROSS THE 8TH DIMENSION aka BUCKAROO BANZAI

1984

DIRECTOR: W. D. Richter.

SCREENPLAY: Earl Mac Rauch.

CAST: Peter Weller, John Lithgow, Ellen Barkin, Jeff Goldblum, Christopher Lloyd.

Color, PG rated, 102m.

Dr. Buckaroo Banzai (Weller) is a half-Japanese, half-American physicist, neurosurgeon, rock musician, rocket-car racer, and leader of team Banzai, free-lance troubleshooters. Somehow, Banzai crashes his rocket car into the eighth dimension, releasing evil aliens. But forget the incoherent plot. Forget Buckaroo Banzai. This movie belongs to John Lithgow as the alien mastermind, Lord John Whorfin, aka Professor Emilio Lizardo, one of the screen's most memorable villains. His attempt to escape in his malfunctioning spaceship while browbeating his crew, is hysterical. Even his feet are funny! This was screenwriter Richter's directing debut.

AKIRA KUROSAWA'S DREAMS

1990

DIRECTOR: Akira Kurosawa.

SCREENPLAY: Akira Kurosawa.

CAST: Mitsuko Baisho, Toshihiko Nakano, Mitsunori Isaki, Mieko Harada, Akira Terao, Martin Scorsese.

Color, PG rated, 119m.

A young boy witnesses a secret ceremony in the woods, the spirits of a peach orchard come to life in dazzling color, mountain climbers are caught in a blizzard and are enticed by a beguiling female spirit, a young man watches a funeral procession in an idyllic village.... These are some of the eight dream sequences in the 80-year-old Kurosawa's personal, filmed meditation on life and death. The images in this haunting, visually breathtaking film will linger in your memory.

ANDROID

1982

DIRECTOR: Aaron Lipstadt.

SCREENPLAY: James Reigle, Don Opper.

CAST: Klaus Kinski, Brie Howard, Norbert Weisser, Crofton Hardester, Kendra Kirchner, Don Opper.

Color, PG rated, 80m.

Android Max 404 (Opper) likes rock-and-roll music and old movies, and wants to visit earth some day. He's assistant to mad scientist Dr. Daniels (Kinski) who, unbeknownst to Max, is working on a more advanced android to replace him. When the opportunity arises, Max plans his escape in a stolen spaceship. An oddly endearing sci-fi story. Kinski, who died in 1991, did so many movies and stage productions around the world, that no one has yet been able to compile a complete record of his work.

THE BROTHER FROM ANOTHER PLANET

1984

DIRECTOR: John Sayles.

SCREENPLAY: John Sayles.

CAST: Joe Morton, Darryl Edwards, Leonard Jackson, Steve James.

Color, Not rated (language, violence), 108m.

Morton plays an alien whose spaceship crashes in New York harbor near Ellis Island. Tired and disheveled, he winds up in Harlem, where the neighborhood people look after him, thinking he's a mute street person. He amazes them with his talent to heal video arcade games and humans with his touch. Director Sayles gives himself a small, but plum role as a dogged alien cop who's tracking Morton down. Along with the humor, Sayles uses the situation to make some serious comments about the problems of contemporary American cities. In 1983, Sayles won a MacArthur Foundation grant which provided him with money to work for the next five years, and this film was one of the results. All his movies are independently produced.

COLOSSUS: THE FORBIN PROJECT

1969

DIRECTOR: Joseph Sargent.

SCREENPLAY: James Bridges, from the novel by D. F. Jones.

CAST: Eric Braedon, Susan Clark, Gordon Pinsent, William Schallert.

Color, PG rated, 100m.

This is a neat little thriller about a supercomputer that develops the capacity for independent thought and attempts to take over the world. Intelligent and well-made, the movie stars Eric Braedon, unknown at the time, who now plays Victor Newman on the CBS soap *The Young and the Restless.* A bigger name may have brought this movie the attention it deserved.

THE DAY THE EARTH CAUGHT FIRE

1962

DIRECTOR: Val Guest.

SCREENPLAY: Wolf Mankowitz, Val Guest.

CAST: Edward Judd, Janet Munro, Leo McKern.

B&W, Not rated, 95m.

After beginning an investigation into recent weather changes, two London newspaper reporters (McKern and Judd) discover that the U.S. and U.S.S.R. have inadvertently conducted nuclear bomb tests at the same time, sending the earth off its axis and hurtling it toward the sun. Good special effects help create a realistic vision of the effects of the rising heat, including violent storms around the world. Panic and confusion reign as the utilities break down and shortages occur. Michael Caine appears in a bit part as a traffic cop. Val Guest, who produced, directed, and co-wrote the movie, got the idea from reading letters in the *Times* from people who were worried about the effects of nuclear testing on the weather.

DEATH WATCH

1980

DIRECTOR: Bertrand Tavernier.

SCREENPLAY: Bertrand Tavernier, David Rayfiel, from the novel *The Unsleeping Eye* by David Compton.

CAST: Romy Schneider, Harvey Keitel, Harry Dean Stanton, Max von Sydow.

Color, R rated, 128m.

This thoughtful, low-key science fiction story is set in the near future, when death becomes a spectator sport on television. Romy Schneider is a terminally ill woman who's offered money to let Keitel, a reporter who's had a camera implanted in his brain, film her during her last days. Everything he sees appears live on television. She tries to run away, but Keitel

manages to keep track of her as she travels the countryside. A strong statement on the power and intrusiveness of the media.

FAHRENHEIT 451

1967

DIRECTOR: François Truffaut.

SCREENPLAY: François Truffaut, Jean-Louis Richard, from the novel by Ray Bradbury.

CAST: Oscar Werner, Julie Christie, Cyril Cusack, Anton Diffring, Jeremy Spenser, Alex Scott.

Color, Not rated, 112m.

This adaptation of Ray Bradbury's cautionary tale is set in the not-too-distant future, when all books have been banned because they disturb people, making them antisocial and unhappy. Montag (Werner) is a member of the Fire Brigade. His job is to find hidden books and burn them. Christie appears in two roles, as Montag's conformist pill-popping wife, and as a young woman who motivates him to become interested in the books he's destroying. In keeping with the theme of the movie, the opening credits are spoken. The insistent score is by Bernard Herrmann. Truffaut's only English-language film is probably the best screen version done of any of Bradbury's stories.

FANTASTIC PLANET

1973

DIRECTOR: René Laloux.

SCREENPLAY: René Laloux, Roland Topor, from a novel by Stefan Wul.

CAST: Voices of Barry Bostwick, Nora Heflin.

Color, Not rated, 72m.

This animated Franco-Czech production is an allegorical tale about a futuristic planet, where a race of huge, blue humanoid creatures tolerate people as tiny pets for their

children. Periodically, the humanoids are forced to eradicate large numbers of the little pests, so they won't overrun the planet. Visually fascinating, with an intriguing soundtrack, the film is filled with bizarre creatures engaging in even more bizarre behavior.

FAR AWAY, SO CLOSE!

1993

DIRECTOR:	Wim Wenders.
SCREENPLAY:	Wim Wenders, Ulrich Zieger, Richard Reitinger.
CAST:	Otto Sander, Horst Buchholz, Nastassia Kinski, Heinz Ruhmann, Bruno Ganz, Solveig Dommartin, Willem Dafoe. Cameos by Lou Reed, Mikhail Gorbachev, Peter Falk.

Color/B&W, PG-13 rated, 140m. Subtitled.

If you enjoyed *Wings of Desire*, you should certainly seek out this sequel. It's not as good as the original, but it still has a great deal to recommend it. Also set in Berlin, it tells the story of the angel Cassiel (Sander), who wants to follow the example of his friend Damiel (Ganz) and become mortal. He wants to do good works, to correct some of the problems he's watched from above, but he finds that mortal life isn't easy, and he goes astray. Packed with big talent in small roles, this sequel has much of the same lyrical quality, but with more humor and a little lighter feel overall.

FIEND WITHOUT A FACE

1957

DIRECTOR:	Arthur Crabtree.
SCREENPLAY:	Herbert J. Leder, from the short story "The Thought Monster" by Amelia Reynolds.
CAST:	Kynaston Reeves, Terry Kilburn, Marshall Thompson.

B&W, Not rated, 75m.

A new air base has moved into the neighborhood, and the locals fear that it's emitting large doses of radiation because of some unusual deaths in the area. They should worry, but not for the reason they suspect. A professor who's been studying mind control and thought materialization is inadvertently creating brain-sucking creatures out of his subconscious mind. At first, these entities can't be seen, but eventually the writhing, leaping brains become visible, making for a horrifying finale. Exceptionally well done.

THE 5,000 FINGERS OF DR. T

1953

DIRECTOR: Roy Rowland.

SCREENPLAY: Dr. Seuss (Theodore Geisel), Alan Scott.

CAST: Hans Conried, Tommy Rettig, Peter Lind Hayes, Mary Healy.

Color, Not rated, 88m.

Rettig would rather play baseball than practice the piano, and he hates his demanding piano teacher, Dr. Terwilliker, so much, he has nightmares about him. This wonderfully surreal fantasy was rejected by audiences at the time and has been largely ignored since. A reason may be that although it was presumably released for children, the sophisticated dream sequences are really a delight for adults, and may put kids off music lessons altogether. This is surely one of the most unusual mainstream movies ever made, and was probably Conried's best role. Academy Award nominee for its score by Frederick Hollander.

THE HANDMAID'S TALE

1990

DIRECTOR: Volker Schlöndorff.

SCREENPLAY: Harold Pinter, from the novel by Margaret Atwood.

CAST: Natasha Richardson, Robert Duvall, Faye Dunaway, Aidan Quinn, Elizabeth McGovern, Victoria Tennant.

Color, R rated, 109m.

Described as a “feminist horror story,” this grim tale, set in the near future, presents a society where most women have been left sterile from chemical pollution. The few fertile women remaining are brainwashed, and ordered by the ultra-conservative government to bear children for the elite members of the population. Richardson is one of these women, and she’s assigned to a home where she has to deal with jealous wife Dunaway and avoid husband Duvall. A chilling story, well told.

THE HIDDEN

1987

DIRECTOR: Jack Sholder.

SCREENPLAY: Bob Hunt.

CAST: Michael Nouri, Kyle MacLachlan, Ed O’Ross, Clu Gulager, Claudia Christian.

Color, R rated, 90m.

A parasitic alien is turning ordinary people into psychotic killers with two things in common, a taste for Ferraris and heavy metal music. Disguised as an FBI agent, good-guy alien MacLachlan joins L.A. cop Nouri on its trail. Nouri thinks there’s something a little weird about this guy, but he can’t put his finger on it. From the opening high-speed car chase, this violent little sci-fi thriller careens off at full-throttle and never lets up.

ICEMAN

1984

DIRECTOR: Fred Schepisi.

SCREENPLAY: Chip Proser, John Drimmer, from a story by Drimmer.

CAST: Timothy Hutton, John Lone, Lindsay Crouse, Josef Sommer, Danny Glover.

Color, PG rated, 99m.

A prehistoric man, frozen in a glacier for 40,000 years, is found by an oil-drilling company and thawed out. When he revives, he's terrified by the world he sees, and Lone does a superb job of conveying this primitive man's emotions with his eyes. Hutton is the humanist scientist who wants to treat him like a man, not a scientific curiosity. Director Schepisi (*A Cry in the Dark, Six Degrees of Separation*) once again shows his versatility, and he gets excellent support from his long-time associates, composer Bruce Smeaton and cinematographer Ian Baker.

IT CAME FROM OUTER SPACE

1953

DIRECTOR: Jack Arnold.

SCREENPLAY: Harry Essex, from *The Meteor* by Ray Bradbury.

CAST: Richard Carlson, Barbara Rush, Charles Drake, Kathleen Hughes.

B&W, Not rated, 80m.

Amateur astronomer and writer Carlson sees something streak across the sky and crash into the Arizona desert near his home. He finds an alien spaceship, but before he can show it to anyone, it's buried in an avalanche, and no one believes him. This was the first movie to use the idea of aliens taking over human bodies, and it's one of the best of its kind. Director Arnold, who made *The Creature from the Black Lagoon* the following year, believed in getting the audience involved by setting the mood, so he shot as much of the film as possible in the desert, instead of in the studio.

THE MAN IN THE WHITE SUIT

1951

DIRECTOR: Alexander Mackendrick.

SCREENPLAY: Roger Macdougall, John Dighton, Alexander Mackendrick.

CAST: Alec Guinness, Joan Greenwood, Cecil Parker, Vida Hope, Ernest Thesiger, Michael Gough, Howard Marion Crawford, Miles Malleson, George Benson, Edie Martin.

Color, Not rated, 81m.

In this science-fiction comedy, Guinness plays a brilliant amateur scientist who's dangerously impatient. He takes menial jobs at textile companies to have access to their research laboratories at night, so he may pursue his dream of inventing a fabric that will never soil or wear out. Inevitably, something blows up, and he moves on to another company. The whimsical, rhythmic sound effects for his experiments are so appealing, they were marketed as "The White Suit Samba." A sterling cast is headed by the ever-brilliant Guinness and Joan Greenwood.

MIRACLE MILE

1989

DIRECTOR: Steve DeJarnatt.

SCREENPLAY: Steve DeJarnatt.

CAST: Anthony Edwards, Mare Winningham, John Agar, Lou Hancock, Mykel T. Williamson.

Color, R rated, 88m.

Edwards is at an L.A. coffee shop in the middle of the night when the pay phone outside starts to ring, in this variation on the question, "What would you do if...?" When he answers the phone, he's told in very convincing terms that a nuclear attack has been launched, and that L.A. will be hit in about an hour. What follows is a thrilling high-speed race against the clock as he tries to get his girlfriend and family

out of town before it's too late. This is a fun ride, full of action and suspense. Music by Tangerine Dream.

THE NAVIGATOR: A MEDIEVAL ODYSSEY

1988

DIRECTOR: Vincent Ward.

SCREENPLAY: Vincent Ward, Kely Lyons, Geoff Chapple.

CAST: Bruce Lyons, Chris Haywood, Hamish McFarlane, Marshall Napier, Noel Appleby.

B&W/Color, PG rated, 92m.

During the Black Death of the 14th century, a group of peasants, led by a psychic boy, make a pilgrimage through a tunnel in the earth and emerge into the 20th century. This strange new world they discover is filled with danger, and even crossing the road becomes a perilous undertaking. This highly original time-travel fantasy from New Zealand was made on a shoestring, but it creates an authentic evocation of the Middle Ages that adds to a big-budget look. It boasts strong, believable performances and a moody, dark atmosphere. Score by Davood A. Tabrizi.

PAPERHOUSE

1990

DIRECTOR: Bernard Rose.

SCREENPLAY: Matthew Jacobs.

CAST: Charlotte Burke, Ben Cross, Glenne Headley, Elliott Spears, Gemma Jones.

Color, PG-13 rated, 92m.

After drawing pictures of a house, an 11-year-old girl starts having vivid dreams about going to the house and finding a boy trapped there. When her family doctor tells her about a patient of hers who's very ill, the girl believes that it's the boy in her dreams, and that her drawings are affecting the boy's real life. This is an unusual combination of psychological drama and haunting fantasy that is enchanting and sometimes horrifying. The well-crafted dream sequences have an eerie and ominous feeling, and the film builds slowly to a spellbinding conclusion. This was a strong feature debut for director Rose. Score by Hans Zimmer and Stanley Myers.

PICNIC AT HANGING ROCK

1975

DIRECTOR: Peter Weir.

SCREENPLAY: Cliff Green, from the novel by Joan Lindsay.

CAST: Rachel Roberts, Dominic Guard, Helen Morse, Jacki Weaver, Vivean Gray.

Color, PG rated, 110m.

At the turn of the century, a group of schoolgirls and their teacher take a picnic in a remote, rocky landscape, and several of the girls vanish, never to be found. Director Weir (*Witness, Dead Poet's Society*) has the exceptional ability to create an atmosphere of foreboding and disquiet in a seemingly ordinary setting, and the film has a mysterious, haunting mood. Pan flutist Zamfir provides the mesmerizing music.

THE QUIET EARTH

1985

DIRECTOR: Geoff Murphy.

SCREENPLAY: Bill Baer, Bruno Lawrence, Sam Pillsbury.

CAST: Bruno Lawrence, Alison Routledge, Peter Smith.

Color, R rated, 91m.

A scientist (Lawrence) who attempts suicide with pills wakes up to discover that he's completely alone. There isn't one living creature that he can find, although everything else is intact. After an initial fling with all the modern world's toys at his disposal, he becomes terrified with the implications of his situation. This is the intriguing premise of this low-key

but suspenseful sci-fi thriller from New Zealand. It gives a wonderful sense of what this vast world would be like without people, with the help of James Bartle's splendid cinematography. Distinct and well done.

THE RAPTURE

1991

DIRECTOR: Michael Tolkin.

SCREENPLAY: Michael Tolkin.

CAST: Mimi Rogers, Patrick Bauchau, David Duchovny, Kimberly Cullum, Will Patton.

Color, R rated, 102m.

Rogers gives the best performance of her career as a bored, promiscuous woman whose life seems purposeless until she joins a fundamentalist Christian church, marries a devout man, and has a daughter. After her husband is murdered, Rogers begins to have religious visions about the end of the world and takes her daughter to the desert to await the final judgment. Intense and disturbing, this dark fantasy explores some of the more forbidding aspects of religious faith. This first directing effort by writer Tolkin (*The Player*) is provocative, vivid, and compelling.

THE SEVEN FACES OF DR. LAO

1964

DIRECTOR: George Pal.

SCREENPLAY: Charles Beaumont, from the novel *The Circus of Dr. Lao* by Charles G. Finney.

CAST: Tony Randall, Arthur O'Connell, John Ericson, Barbara Eden, Noah Beery Jr., Lee Patrick, Minerva Urecal, John Qualen.

Color, Not rated, 100m.

Randall has a field day as the inscrutable Dr. Lao, an old Chinese gentleman whose traveling circus comes to a small western town and helps solve its problems. With a colorful

circus atmosphere, this endearing fantasy is built around Randall's imaginative portrayal of six different characters in elaborate disguise. The spectacular makeup effects won a special Oscar for their creator, William Tuttle.

STRANGE INVADERS

1983

DIRECTOR:	Michael Laughlin.
SCREENPLAY:	William Condon, Michael Laughlin.
CAST:	Paul LeMat, Nancy Allen, Diana Scarwid, Michael Lerner, Louise Fletcher, Wallace Shawn.

Color, PG rated, 94m.

In 1958, Centerville, Illinois is invaded by aliens who take over the local residents' bodies to disguise their hideousness. Twenty-five years later, New York professor LeMat finds out his ex-wife (Scarwid) is one of those aliens and she's going to take their daughter with her when she leaves earth. This send-up of '50s alien-possession movies has some good laughs, but it also works very well as a straightforward sci-fi thriller which builds to an exciting climax. The aliens are truly menacing and the makeup effects are excellent. The rousing score is by John Addison.

THIS ISLAND EARTH

1955

DIRECTOR:	Joseph Newman.
SCREENPLAY:	Franklin Coen, Edwrd G. O'Callaghan, from the novel by Raymond F. Jones.
CAST:	Jeff Morrow, Faith Domergue, Rex Reason, Lance Fuller.

B&W, Not rated, 86m.

Aliens from planet Metaluna are kidnapping scientists from Earth to help them defend their planet against the Zahgons. Alien Exeter (Morrow), disguising himself as an earthling

(not too well, one might add), recruits scientists for a mysterious secret project. What they don't know is that they'll be taken to Metaluna to help that planet defend itself against the evil Zahgons. Sounds pretty silly, but there's some exciting action, and the special effects on Metaluna are impressive.

THE TIN DRUM

1979

DIRECTOR: Volker Schlöndorff.

SCREENPLAY: Jean-Claude Carriere, Volker Schlöndorff, from the novel by Günter Grass.

CAST: David Bennent, Mario Adorf, Angela Winkler, Daniel Olbrychski.

Color, R rated, 140m. Subtitled.

Distrustful of the adult world, little Oskar decides, at age three, to stop growing. He's inseparable from his tin drum, on which he beats out his anger. If someone tries to take it from him, his screams of outrage can shatter glass. The astonishing 12-year-old Bennent gives a disturbing, unforgettable performance as the perpetual three-year-old. Set in post-World War I Germany, during the rise and fall of Naziism, this riveting adaptation of the Günter Grass novel of "outraged innocence" won an Oscar as Best Foreign Language Film.

20 MILLION MILES TO EARTH

1957

DIRECTOR: Nathan Juran.

SCREENPLAY: Bob Williams, Christopher Knopf.

CAST: William Hopper, Joan Taylor, Frank Puglia, Thomas Browne Henry.

B&W, Not rated, 82m.

On its return from Venus, a manned spacecraft crashes into the waters off Sicily. The captain of the ship (Hopper) survives, as does an egg, which soon hatches into a mythical-looking beast that grows quickly into a monster. Hopper leads the chase as the creature makes his way to Rome, running amok until it's finally cornered in the Coliseum. Good suspense and effects make this one of the best "monster on the loose" movies, featuring some of Ray Harryhausen's most convincing special effects.

WAR OF THE WORLDS

1953

DIRECTOR: Byron Haskin.

SCREENPLAY: Barre Lyndon, from the novel by H. G. Wells.

CAST: Gene Barry, Les Tremayne, Ann Robinson, Robert Cornthwaite.

Color, Not rated, 85m.

Ignore the acting in this colorful screen version of the H. G. Wells classic about a Martian invasion of Earth. The menacing, unstoppable Martian battleships steal the show as they roam the countryside, annihilating everything in their path. Even though the budget was minuscule compared to today's sci-fi extravaganzas, the film manages to create some truly frightening effects. There's a wonderfully creepy scene with scientist Barry and librarian Robinson, as they're trapped in an old house surrounded by aliens. Producer George Pal won an Oscar for his special effects, one of the five in his career. Narrated by Sir Cedric Hardwicke.

WINGS OF DESIRE

1987

DIRECTOR: Wim Wenders.

SCREENPLAY: Wim Wenders, Peter Handke.

CAST: Bruno Ganz, Solveig Dommartin, Otto Sander, Curt Bois, Peter Falk.

B&W/Color, PG-13 rated, 127m. Subtitled.

Two angels, Damiel (Ganz) and Cassiel (Sander), float above the city of Berlin, descending invisibly into the streets to listen to the thoughts of passing people, pausing to gently touch the shoulder of a child. Damiel becomes enchanted by an aerialist in a circus (Dommartin), and longs to become mortal, so he can be with her. The poetic meditations of the dialogue reveal the loneliness and separation of the lives these angels watch over with such tender concern, and the cinematography of Henri Alekan and the score by Jürgen Knieper combine to give this masterful film a hypnotic, tranquil quality that is unforgettable.

Horror

THE ABOMINABLE DR. PHIBES

1971

DIRECTOR: Robert Fuest.

SCREENPLAY: James Whiton, William Goldstein.

CAST: Vincent Price, Joseph Cotten, Hugh Griffith, Terry-Thomas, Peter Jeffrey, Virginia North.

Color, Not rated, 94m.

A disfigured doctor seeks vengeance after his wife dies on the operating table. He goes after the ten doctors involved in the operation in gruesomely imaginative ways, according to the ten curses of the Pharoahs: boils, bats, frogs, blood, rats, hail, beasts, locusts, darkness, and death of the firstborn. Joseph Cotten, the doctor who was in charge of the operation when his wife died, is left for last. With art deco set design and costumes, this is a great-looking combination of camp humor and horror. Fuest was the director of the popular British TV series *The Avengers.*

ALLIGATOR

1980

DIRECTOR: Lewis Teague.

SCREENPLAY: John Sayles.

CAST: Robert Forster, Robin Ryker, Michael Gazzo, Dean Jagger, Jack Carter, Henry Silva.

Color, R rated, 94m.

A baby alligator, flushed down the toilet in Chicago, grows to enormous size in the sewers and terrorizes the city. This urban myth come to life is an entertaining horror-comedy from an ingenious John Sayles script that's a mix of jokes and frights. Cop Forster is trying his best to corral the monster with the aid of Silva, who's a standout as a macho alligator hunter. Lots of gags sprinkled throughout, including some well-placed graffiti.

ASYLUM

1972

DIRECTOR:	Roy Ward Baker.
SCREENPLAY:	Robert Bloch.
CAST:	Patrick Magee, Robert Powell, Geoffrey Bayldon, Barbara Parkins, Sylvia Syms, Richard Todd, Peter Cushing, Barry Morse, Britt Ekland, Charlotte Rampling, Herbert Lom.

Color, PG rated, 88m.

This horror anthology features Powell as a young psychiatrist seeking work at an insane asylum. He's given four patients to evaluate as a test to see if he can determine which is a former psychiatrist who's gone mad. Each patient has a chilling tale to tell that explains what caused their breakdowns. An enjoyable collection, which builds to a satisfyingly shocking conclusion. The screenplay is by Robert Bloch, best known as the author of *Psycho*.

THE BODY SNATCHER

1945

DIRECTOR:	Robert Wise.
SCREENPLAY:	Philip MacDonald, Carlos Keith, from the story by Robert Louis Stevenson.
CAST:	Boris Karloff, Henry Daniell, Bela Lugosi, Edith Atwater.

B&W, Not rated, 77m.

Set in 1831 Edinburgh, Karloff plays a sinister grave robber and murderer who supplies cadavers for physician Daniell's anatomy classes. The well-meaning doctor is dedicated to his research and doesn't ask too many questions of the loathesome Karloff, who's also blackmailing him. Karloff is excellent as the sadistic character who drives Daniell over the brink, and he displays what an accomplished actor he is when given a good part. Lugosi appears in a small part as the doctor's servant, and he and Karloff have a couple of choice scenes together. The story by Robert Louis Stevenson was inspired by the real-life case of the murderous grave robbers Burke and Hare.

BRAIN DAMAGE

1988

DIRECTOR:	Frank Henenlotter.
SCREENPLAY:	Frank Henenlotter.
CAST:	Rick Herbst, Gordon MacDonald, Jennifer Lowry, Theo Barnes.

Color, R rated, 89m.

From the creator of *Basket Case* comes Aylmer, a wisecracking, sluglike parasite who spends most of his time resting in a bucket of water, but who requires a human host to help keep him alive. He gets them to do his bidding by attaching himself to the back of their neck and injecting a hallucinatory drug into their brain. It produces such an exhilarating high that they'll do whatever he asks of them. The similarity between Aylmer's enslavement of his human host to drug addiction is no coincidence in this gory comedy. The scenes between Aylmer and his host (Herbst) when they're squabbling are hilarious.

CARNIVAL OF SOULS

1962

DIRECTOR: Herk Harvey.

SCREENPLAY: John Clifford.

CAST: Candace Hilligoss, Herk Harvey, Francis Feist, Sidney Berger.

B&W, Not rated, 80m.

After surviving a car crash in which her friends are killed, a young Kansas woman takes a job as a church organist in Utah, and becomes haunted by an eerie presence. Her life starts unraveling, and she finds herself being drawn to an old abandoned amusement park outside of town. Shot for next to nothing in Kansas, this is a delightfully creepy ghost story. Complete with spooky organ music, it has an authentic weirdness to it that's unique.

THE CHANGELING

1979

DIRECTOR: Peter Medak.

SCREENPLAY: William Gray, Diana Maddox.

CAST: George C. Scott, Melvyn Douglas, Trish Van Devere, John Colicos, Jean Marsh, Barry Morse.

Color, R rated, 107m.

After losing his wife and child in a car accident, composer Scott moves from New York to Seattle to take a university teaching job. He leases a Victorian mansion where he can compose in peace, but he's soon disturbed by the sound of running water and loud, metallic banging. After investigating the house's history, he comes to the conclusion that it is haunted by the spirit of a murdered child. This very effective hair-raiser is highlighted by one of the most chilling séances ever.

THE CONQUEROR WORM
aka **WITCHFINDER GENERAL**

1968

DIRECTOR: Michael Reeves.

SCREENPLAY: Michael Reeves, Tom Baker.

CAST: Vincent Price, Rupert Davies, Ian Ogilvy, Patrick Wymark, Hilary Dwyer, Wilfred Brambell.

Color, Not rated (contains violence, torture, nudity), 87m.

This tale, set during the witch hunts in 17th-century England, is all the more horrifying because it's a factual account, based on a real person. Matthew Hopkins made his living traveling the countryside, torturing confessions of witchcraft out of innocent villagers. Price delivers one of the best performances of his career by playing this sadistic psychopath absolutely straight. The graphic scenes of torture are all the harder to stomach because of their authenticity.

CRONOS

1992

DIRECTOR: Guillermo Del Toro.

SCREENPLAY: Guillermo Del Toro.

CAST: Federico Luppi, Ron Perlman, Claudio Brook, Margarita Isabel, Tamara Shanath.

Color, R rated, 92m. Subtitled and English.

The Cronos device, invented by a 15th-century alchemist, gives eternal life to its possessors, but for a price. They turn into vampires of sorts, craving human blood. Antique-shop owner Luppi finds the device hidden in a statue and discovers its horrible secret. Dying recluse Brook wants the device and sends Perlman to get it at any cost. Filmed in Mexico, this is a well-made combination of horror and humor, with good special effects. Satisfying score by Javier Alvarez.

CURSE OF THE DEMON
aka **NIGHT OF THE DEMON**

1957

DIRECTOR: Jacques Tourneur.

SCREENPLAY: Charles Bennett, Hal E. Chester, from the story "Casting the Runes" by M. R. James.

CAST: Dana Andrews, Peggy Cummins, Niall MacGinnis, Athene Seyler, Brian Wilde, Maurice Denham.

B&W, Not rated, 87m.

The opening shots of a man running madly through the mist-filled woods set the tone for this story of a psychologist (Andrews) who inadvertently runs afoul of a Satanist while investigating the death of a colleague. This great-looking, atmospheric thriller boasts an intelligent script and striking visual effects, including a thoroughly nasty demon.

DEAD OF NIGHT

1945

DIRECTOR: Cavalcanti, Charles Crichton, Basil Dearden, Robert Hamer.

SCREENPLAY: John Baines, Angus MacPhail.

CAST: Mervyn Johns, Roland Culver, Michael Redgrave, Antony Baird, Judy Kelly, Miles Malleson, Sally Ann Howes.

B&W, Not rated, 102m.

A young architect (Johns) fears that his recurrent, murderous nightmare is coming true when he's summoned to an English country mansion that seems strangely familiar. This classic horror anthology features five stories of the supernatural as told by the people he meets there. The last story, directed by Cavalcanti, features Michael Redgrave's sensational performance as a ventriloquist who's tormented by his dummy. Often imitated, it's never been improved on. The seemingly unrelated stories are all cleverly brought together in the rip-

snorting finale. Horror films were banned in England during World War II, and this was the first one to be released after the war.

DEAD RINGERS

1988

DIRECTOR:	David Cronenberg.
SCREENPLAY:	David Cronenberg, Norman Snider, from the book *Twins* by Barry Wood.
CAST:	Jeremy Irons, Genevieve Bujold, Heidi Von Palleske, Barbara Gordon, Shirley Douglas.

Color, R rated, 115m.

Irons gives a bravura performance as gynecologist twin brothers who confuse their identities and gradually descend into depravity and madness in this fact-based biological horror story. Bujold is excellent as the patient and lover of one of the brothers. Complete with gory scenes of surgery done with menacingly perverse surgical instruments, the film is directed with gruesome style by David Cronenberg, who once again goes into uncomfortable territory with this exploration of the horror of the body and sexual dread.

THE DEAD ZONE

1983

DIRECTOR:	David Cronenberg.
SCREENPLAY:	Jeffrey Boam, from the novel by Stephen King.
CAST:	Christopher Walken, Brooke Adams, Tom Skerritt, Herbert Lom, Anthony Zerbe, Colleen Dewhurst.

Color, R rated, 103m.

After lying in a coma for five years after a car accident, teacher Walken wakes up with the ability to see the future of anyone he touches. In an attempt to escape these flashes of impending tragedy, he withdraws from human contact until he reluctantly agrees to help Sheriff Skerritt with a murder investigation. Walken's affecting performance as the tormented young man who is compelled to try to change the future is one of his best, and the film benefits from an excellent supporting cast and confident direction by Cronenberg.

DRACULA'S DAUGHTER

1936

DIRECTOR: Lambert Hillyer.

SCREENPLAY: Garrett Fort.

CAST: Gloria Holden, Otto Kruger, Marguerite Churchill, Edward Van Sloan, Irving Pichel, Nan Grey, Hedda Hopper.

B&W, Not rated, 70m.

Gloria Holden is Countess Dracula, daughter of the infamous vampire, who follows her father's body to England after Von Helsing (Van Sloan) finishes him off. She steals his body from the morgue and burns it in an attempt to free herself from the family curse, but to no avail. She even consults with a psychiatrist (Kruger). The sensual countess was the best-known role of former model Holden, who specialized in playing femmes fatales. Well-plotted, with a haunting, detached aura, the film was unfortunately a box-office failure.

EYES WITHOUT A FACE
aka **THE HORROR CHAMBER OF DR. FAUSTUS**

1959

DIRECTOR: George Franju.

SCREENPLAY: Jean Redon, from his novel.

CAST: Pierre Brasseur, Alida Valli, Edith Scob, François Guérin.

B&W, Not rated, 90m. Subtitled.

A famous plastic surgeon (Brasseur) feels responsible for the car accident that horribly disfigures his daughter's face. She must wear a china mask, and her eyes are her only means of expression. Consumed with guilt, Brasseur enlists the aid of his mistress (Valli) to kidnap beautiful girls so he can surgically transfer their faces onto his daughter, but the skin won't heal. This elegant, stylish production boasts elaborate sets and costumes, and includes very realistic scenes of surgery. Director Franju describes it as a "poetic fantasy." Released in the U.S. as *The Horror Chamber of Dr. Faustus*. Music by Maurice Jarre.

THE HAUNTED PALACE

1963

DIRECTOR: Roger Corman.

SCREENPLAY: Charles Beaumont.

CAST: Vincent Price, Debra Paget, Lon Chaney Jr., Frank Maxwell, Elisha Cook Jr., Leo Gordon.

Color, Not rated, 85m.

In 1875, Price and his wife, Paget, come to a small New England town where he's inherited a mansion. His ancestor, who was burned as a warlock, takes possession of his body in order to exact revenge on the town. Price gives an unusually understated performance as the mild-mannered man and his demented ancestor. With a brooding, creepy atmosphere, this is also one of Corman's best films. The title is taken from a poem by Edgar Allan Poe, but the story is from the H. P. Lovecraft story "The Case of Charles Dexter Ward."

THE HAUNTING

1963

DIRECTOR: Robert Wise.

SCREENPLAY: Nelson Gidding.

CAST: Julie Harris, Claire Bloom, Richard Johnson, Russ Tamblyn, Lois Maxwell, Fay Compton.

B&W, Not rated, 112m.

One of the best of its kind, this chiller delivers its goosebumps without gore. The story, based on the novel *The Haunting of Hill House* by Shirley Jackson, involves a small group of people who are brought together to investigate alleged supernatural occurrences in an old New England mansion. Harris plays a disturbed young woman who becomes the victim of the house's evil spell. Wise creates a creepy, unnerving atmosphere that keeps you off-guard. Don't be deceived by the lack of bloodshed in this one; it's as frightening as anything you're ever likely to see. Filmed in England.

I WALKED WITH A ZOMBIE

1943

DIRECTOR: Jacques Tourneur.

SCREENPLAY: Curt Siodmak, Ardel Wray, from a story by Inez Wallace.

CAST: Frances Dee, Tom Conway, James Ellison, Edith Barrett, Christine Gordon.

B&W, Not rated, 69m.

TOM DISCH

Les Cousins (1958) and **This Man Must Die** (1970), both by Claude Chabrol.

Judex (1960) and **Les Yeux Sans Visage** (1963), both by Georges Franju.

Out of the Past (1947), directed by Jacques Tourneur, with Robert Mitchum and Kirk Douglas.

Tom Disch writes criticism for *The Nation* and is the author of the novels *The Priest* and *The M. D.* He lives in New York.

The plot is borrowed from *Jane Eyre* for this atmospheric tale of a nurse (Dee) who travels to a Caribbean island to care for the wife of plantation owner Conway. Doctors believe the wife (Gordon) is in her trancelike state as a result of a serious illness, but the locals know that she's really a zombie. The house is airy and open, and the openness of it is what makes it feel so vulnerable at night as Gordon rises and wanders about like a ghost. The mood is eerie due to the effective night photography of J. Roy Hunt, and the voodoo drums can always be heard in the distance. The movie builds to a final voodoo scene that is amazingly effective.

ISLAND OF LOST SOULS

1932

DIRECTOR: Erle C. Kenton.

SCREENPLAY: Waldemar Young, Philip Wylie, from *The Island of Dr. Moreau* by H. G. Wells.

CAST: Charles Laughton, Bela Lugosi, Richard Arlen, Kathleen Burke, Leila Hyams.

B&W, Not rated, 74m.

This is one of the most successful versions of the oft-filmed *The Island of Dr. Moreau,* with Charles Laughton a deliciously lurid villain as the evil doctor who conducts unholy experiments on his remote island. Lugosi is the leader of the half-beast, half-human natives who are the unfortunate results of his experiments in the "House of Pain." The claustrophobic and menacing jungle add to the nightmarish atmosphere. This film is the source for the now famous lines, "The natives are restless," and "Are we not men?"

KWAIDAN

1964

DIRECTOR: Masaki Kobayashi.

SCREENPLAY: Yoko Mizuki.

CAST: Rentaro Mikuni, Ganjiro Nakamura, Katsuo Nakamura, Michiyo Aratama, Misako Watanabe, Keiko Kishi.

Color, Not rated, 164m. Subtitled.

Each of the four exquisitely photographed, ghostly tales in this anthology stand alone. The stories, "The Black Hair," "Woman of the Snow," "Hoichi the Earless," and "In a Cup of Tea," are adapted from stories by Lafcadio Hearn, an American writer who lived in Japan in the late 1800s. The film took many years to complete, and at the time was the most expensive movie ever made in Japan. It shows, in the fabulous sets and its spectacular images. "Kwaidan" in Japanese means "ghost story." The stunning cinematography is by Yoshio Miyajima, and the unsettling score by Tohru Takemitsu. The director, who was a prisoner of war during most of World War II, is best known for his masterpiece *Harakiri.*

MOTEL HELL

1980

DIRECTOR: Kevin Connor.

SCREENPLAY: Robert Jaffe, Steven-Charles Jaffe.

CAST: Rory Calhoun, Paul Linke, Nancy Parsons, Nina Axelrod, Wolfman Jack.

Color, R rated, 92m.

Farmer Vincent and sister Ida sell savory spicy sausage, but what their appreciative customers don't know is that the secret ingredient is the motel guests that they've planted in the garden. This silly spoof of the blood-and-guts horror movies of the '70s comes complete with a chain saw duel amidst the meat hooks. The appropriate title comes from the "o" in Motel Hello being burned out. Not exactly acclaimed by mainstream critics, but horror fans should give it a thumbs-up. Calhoun (Uncle Vincent) is best known for his roles in Westerns.

NEAR DARK

1987

DIRECTOR:	Kathryn Bigelow.
SCREENPLAY:	Eric Red, Kathryn Bigelow.
CAST:	Adrian Pasdar, Jenny Wright, Lance Henriksen, Bill Paxton, Jenette Goldstein, Joshua Miller.

Color, R rated, 94m.

Caleb (Pasdar) discovers too late that the attractive young woman he's just met is a vampire, and he reluctantly joins her roving band of bloodsuckers as they travel through the West in their van, leaving a path of bodies and destruction. Is there any escape? There's nothing romantic about these undead; they enjoy intimidating and torturing their victims before they kill them, and Paxton plays a sadistic, arrogant member of this murderous band with bravado. Miller, who plays the youngest vampire of the "family," will make your flesh crawl. Music by Tangerine Dream. Henriksen, Paxton, and Goldstein were all in *Aliens*.

NOSFERATU

1979

DIRECTOR:	Werner Herzog.
SCREENPLAY:	Werner Herzog.
CAST:	Klaus Kinski, Isabelle Adjani, Bruno Ganz, Walter Ladengast, Roland Topor, Dan Van Husen.

Color, PG rated, 107m. Subtitled.

Herzog's version of the famous vampire story pays homage to the 1922 Murnau classic of the same name. Kinski gives a masterful performance as Count Dracula. Wary as a cat, speaking in soft, low tones, he's an eerie, almost pitiful, creature. Beautifully photographed by Jörg Schmidt-Reitwein, the film is wonderfully creepy, capturing a somewhat rancid quality in the air. Effective use of music by Popul Vuh, Florian Fricke, Richard Wagner, and Charles Gounod.

PARENTS

1989

DIRECTOR: Bob Balaban.

SCREENPLAY: Christopher Hawthorne.

CAST: Randy Quaid, Mary Beth Hurt, Sandy Dennis, Bryan Madorsky.

Color, R rated, 82m.

In this 1950s suburban nightmare, 10-year-old Michael feels he's a disappointment to his looming and somewhat greasy father (Quaid) and his prim and distant mother (Hurt). They pester him constantly about his manners, and he's such a picky eater. Lately, he's been having disturbing dreams about what they do when he's in bed at night. Sandy Dennis is hysterical as the school counselor who takes him under her wing. This truly frightening, horror black-comedy captures the real terror of '50s decor and clothes, in brilliant color. This was actor Balaban's directing debut.

PEEPING TOM

1959

DIRECTOR: Michael Powell.

SCREENPLAY: Leo Marks.

CAST: Carl Boehm, Moira Shearer, Anna Massey, Maxine Audley, Esmond Knight, Michael Goodliffe, Shirley Ann Field, Jack Watson.

Color, Not rated (violence), 109m.

Boehm plays a young man working as a focus puller for a movie company, whose part-time job is taking cheesecake photos. As a child, he was subjected to experiments in fear by his father, who filmed them. Now an adult, he's a psychopath who murders attractive young women while filming the fear on their faces. This film angered critics and audi-

ences alike when it was released, but now, even though it retains its power to shock, it's considered a minor masterpiece, made with great attention to detail and the brilliant color which marked Powell's work. The controversy over the movie virtually ended the career of a major director, who also made *The Red Shoes* and *Black Narcissus,* among others.

Q

1982

DIRECTOR: Larry Cohen.

SCREENPLAY: Larry Cohen.

CAST: Michael Moriarty, Candy Clark, David Carradine, Richard Roundtree, James Dixon.

Color, R rated, 93m.

A flying-serpent incarnation of the ancient Aztec god Quetzalcoatl takes up residence on top of the Chrysler Building and starts knocking off the locals, raining body parts down on the streets below. Moriarty is a standout as jazz musician Jimmy Quinn, a fruitcake who wants the police to pay him to divulge the location of the nest, which he discovered accidentally. This tongue-in-cheek variation on the "monster on the loose" is full of appropriately grisly effects and goofy dark humor. Moriarty is an accomplished jazz musician in real life. Cohen is the director of *It's Alive.*

REPULSION

1965

DIRECTOR: Roman Polanski.

SCREENPLAY: Roman Polanski, Gerrard Brach.

CAST: Catherine Deneuve, Ian Hendry, John Fraser, Patrick Wymark, Yvonne Furneaux.

B&W, Not rated (violence), 105m.

In a role that established that she could act, Deneuve plays a young Belgian manicurist living in London who descends into madness. Left alone in her apartment, she starts having terrifying hallucinations that the walls are ripping open and hands are grabbing at her. When two unfortunate men manage to get in, she murders them viciously with a razor. This amazing portrait of insanity, horrific in its graphic violence, will set your nerves on edge as it builds an almost unbearable tension. Made in England, before Polanski made his first American hit, *Rosemary's Baby,* in 1968.

THE SENDER

1982

DIRECTOR: Roger Christian.

SCREENPLAY: Thomas Baum.

CAST: Kathryn Harrold, Zeljko Ivanek, Shirley Knight, Paul Freeman.

Color, R rated, 91m.

After a suicide attempt, a young man (Ivanek) is admitted to a mental hospital, where it's discovered that his uncontrolled telepathic powers are unleashing his violent nightmares on his psychiatrist (Harrold) and the other patients. His mother seems only interested in getting him back home, and Harrold suspects that she knows more than she's saying. This low-key thriller from England has an original story, good visual effects, and some very scary moments. Atmospheric score by Trevor Jones.

THE STEPFATHER

1986

DIRECTOR: Joseph Ruben.

SCREENPLAY: Donald E. Westlake.

CAST: Terry O'Quinn, Jill Schoelen, Shelley Hack, Charles Lanyer.

Color, R rated, 88m.

From the moment Jerry Blake (O'Quinn) starts dating her mother (Hack), he makes 16-year-old Stephanie's flesh crawl.

But why? Jerry just wants to be the father of a perfect family. He wants to be Ward Cleaver, and on the surface that's exactly what he seems to be. It's the familiar surroundings of suburbia that give this movie its real horror, because nice guy Jerry deals with the shortcomings of his stepfamilies by murdering them and moving on to the next. It's O'Quinn's bone-chilling performance as the psychopath behind the normal facade that elevates this above-the-usual horror fare. Followed by two forgettable sequels. Ruben also directed *Dreamscape.*

THE UNINVITED

1944

DIRECTOR:	Lewis Allen.
SCREENPLAY:	Dodie Smith, Frank Partos, from the novel *Uneasy Freehold* by Dorothy Macardle.
CAST:	Ray Milland, Ruth Hussey, Donald Crisp, Gail Russell, Cornelia Otis Skinner.

B&W, Not rated, 98m.

Milland and sister, Hussey, feel fortunate to have gotten Windward House, a mansion on the spectacular coast of Cornwall, for such a reasonable price. But they soon discover that the house has a tragic past involving a local girl who grew up there (Russell). One of the best ghost stories ever, this atmospheric tale won an Oscar nomination for its extraordinary cinematography by Charles Lang, Jr. The ghostly visual effects, including wilting flowers and pages turning by themselves, are excellent. Victor Young composed the song "Stella by Starlight," featured in the film.

THE WICKER MAN

1973

DIRECTOR: Robin Hardy.

SCREENPLAY: Anthony Shaffer.

CAST: Edward Woodward, Britt Ekland, Christopher Lee, Ingrid Pitt, Diane Cilento.

Color, R rated, 103m.

Woodward is a policeman sent to an isolated Scottish island to investigate a child's death after police receive a letter saying the little girl had been murdered. When he gets there, he discovers that under the guise of normalcy, there is a flourishing secret pagan society that is making human sacrifices. The film convincingly conveys Woodward's growing feeling of isolation and helplessness in this menacing and erotically charged atmosphere, and the suspense builds to a shocking ending. Music by Paul Giovanni. Beware of shorter prints.

Musicals

THE COMMITMENTS

1991

DIRECTOR: Alan Parker.

SCREENPLAY: Dick Clement, Ian Le Frenais, Roddy Doyle, from the novel by Roddy Doyle.

CAST: Robert Arkins, Michael Aherne, Angeline Ball, Maria Doyle, Dave Finnegan, Bronagh Gallagher.

Color, R rated, 117m.

Small-time hustler Jimmy (Arkins) wants to put together a soul band in Dublin because, after all, "the Irish are the blacks of Europe." He places ads in newspapers and puts up fliers which attract a stream of applicants of every stripe. What follows is a humorous, and heartwarming look at the trials and tribulations of this fledging band as they get their act together. The cast of nonactors is very appealing, and the abundant music is great.

IT'S ALWAYS FAIR WEATHER

1955

DIRECTOR: Gene Kelly, Stanley Donen.

SCREENPLAY: Betty Comden, Adolph Green.

CAST: Gene Kelly, Dan Dailey, Michael Kidd, Cyd Charisse, Dolores Gray, David Burns.

Color, Not rated, 102m.

Ten years after they part at the end of World War II, three veterans meet again, as they'd sworn to do. What they discover is that they've changed, and they don't even like each other anymore. But they've agreed to have their reunion on a TV show, so they have to make the best of it. Highlights include Dailey's witty satire on advertising jargon, Charisse doing "Baby, You Knock Me Out," and the "Ash Can Dance" with Kelly, Dailey, and Kidd. This could be considered a sequel of sorts to *On the Town,* with Kelly and Donen directing, and Comden and Green supplying the script and songs. But audiences ignored it, even though it may be the more entertaining movie of the two.

JONATHAN YARDLEY

Jazz on a Summer's Day (1960), directed by Bert Stern.

It's Always Fair Weather (1955), directed by Gene Kelly and Stanley Donen.

Beat the Devil (1954), directed by John Huston.

The Garden of the Finzi-Continis (1970), directed by Vittorio De Sica.

Sweet Smell of Success (1957), directed by Alexander Mackendrick.

The Go-Between (1971), directed by Joseph Losey.

Pygmalion (1938), directed by Anthony Asquith and Leslie Howard.

Henry V (1945), directed by Laurence Olivier.

Metropolitan (1935), directed by Richard Boleslawski.

Jonathan Yardley is both the book critic and a columnist for *The Washington Post.* He lives in Baltimore.

THE LAST POLKA

1984

DIRECTOR: John Blanchard.

SCREENPLAY: Eugene Levy, John Candy.

CAST: John Candy, Eugene Levy, Rick Moranis, Catherine O'Hara.

Color, Not rated, 54m.

The Shmenge Brothers, polka meisters from Leutonia, are featured in this pseudodocumentary send-up of *The Last Waltz,* Scorsese's film documenting the last tour of The Band. The SCTV characters Yosh (Candy) and Stan (Levy) are interviewed as they prepare for their last concert together, talking about the people they've met, the trouble they've seen (including the Lemon Sisters scandal), and how they feel about breaking up the band. On stage they play some of their hits, including "Cabbage Rolls and Coffee, M-m-m good!" Hysterically funny.

LILI

1953

DIRECTOR: Charles Walters.

SCREENPLAY: Helen Deutsch, from the novel by Paul Gallico.

CAST: Leslie Caron, Jean-Pierre Aumont, Mel Ferrer, Kurt Kasznar, Zsa Zsa Gabor, Amanda Blake.

Color, Not rated, 81m.

A 16-year-old French orphan, Lili (Caron), joins a carnival and falls in love with the charming magician (Aumont), not knowing that he's already married. Ferrer, a former dancer, is the puppeteer at the carnival who loves Lili, but is too insecure to tell her, so he talks to her through skits he does with her and the puppets. Caron is wonderful in this charming musical fantasy, keeping it from becoming too saccharine or maudlin, and Ferrer is very appealing as the shy puppeteer.

Sweet, colorful, and heartwarming, it's a treat for all ages. The lovely Oscar-winning score by Bronislau Kaper features the song "Hi Lili, Hi Lo." Caron received an Oscar nomination, as did the screenplay, cinematography by Robert Planck, the art direction by Cedric Gibbons, and the direction.

LIPSTICK ON YOUR COLLAR

1993

DIRECTOR: Renny Rye.

SCREENPLAY: Dennis Potter.

CAST: Giles Thomas, Ewan McGregor, Louise Germaine, Douglas Henshall, Roy Hudd.

Color, Not rated (sexual situations, profanity), 360m.

During the Suez crisis of the 1950s, a painfully awkward British army private, Francis (Thomas), is assigned to an intelligence office where he spends his days translating and decoding messages about Russian troop movements in the Middle East. At home, his apartment is directly below his immediate superior's, a loud, obnoxious corporal who lives there with his sexy but abused wife, Louise (Germaine). Francis is infatuated with Louise, however, she's also being pursued by a middle-aged theater organist. Creator Potter has infused the story with songs of the '50s, and the cast breaks into highly stylized musical numbers at the drop of a hat. As with Potter's other projects (*Pennies from Heaven, The Singing Detective*), this fantasy with a cynical bent is a wonderfully creative entertainment. Originally made for British TV.

PENNIES FROM HEAVEN

1981

DIRECTOR: Herbert Ross.

SCREENPLAY: Dennis Potter.

CAST: Steve Martin, Bernadette Peters, Christopher Walken, Jessica Harper, John McMartin, Vernel Bagneris, Tommy Rall.

Color, R rated, 107m.

Dennis Potter has never caught on much in the U.S., but this adaptation by Potter from his British TV miniseries gives a glimpse into his style. A grim story about a sheet music salesman during the Depression is set against dazzling production numbers featuring songs from the period. Steve Martin was working against type in this one and showed a surprising flair for dance, but the dancing of Christopher Walken to "Let's Misbehave" is a revelation. This is not your average movie musical. Dennis Potter received an Oscar nomination for his screenplay.

SILK STOCKINGS

1957

DIRECTOR: Rouben Mamoulian.

SCREENPLAY: Leonard Gershe, Leonard Spigelgass.

CAST: Fred Astaire, Cyd Charisse, Peter Lorre, Janis Paige, George Tobias, Jules Munshin, Joseph Buloff.

Color, Not rated, 117m.

This musical version of the Cold War satire *Ninotchka* features a Cole Porter score, Cyd Charisse in silk stockings, and Fred Astaire singing and dancing, which is plenty. Charisse is a no-nonsense commissar sent to Paris to retrieve wayward composer Buloff, who's been collaborating with Astaire on a new movie. The score features the lovely "All of You," sung and danced by Astaire and Charisse, and the satire on the movie business, "Stereophonic Sound" sung by Janis Paige and Astaire. Lorre and Munshin provide the comic relief as Charisse's bumbling assistants.

STARDUST

1974

DIRECTOR: Michael Apted.

SCREENPLAY: Ray Connolly.

CAST: David Essex, Adam Faith, Larry Hagman, Marty Wilde, Rosalind Ayres, Keith Moon.

Color, R rated, 97m.

In this sequel to *That'll Be the Day,* Essex continues his role as a rock musician who's just starting his rise to stardom. Everything is great at first as he reaps the rewards of popularity, but soon the agents and managers want more. He willingly obliges in his quest to cash in while he can, but eventually the pressure wears him down, and he turns to drugs for escape. Well done and believable, this version of the now familiar story about the downside of the music business hits the mark. An uncanny resemblance to John Lennon's life story.

SUMMER STOCK

1950

DIRECTOR: Charles Walters.

SCREENPLAY: George Wells, Sy Gomberg.

CAST: Judy Garland, Gene Kelly, Eddie Bracken, Marjorie Main, Gloria De Haven, Phil Silvers, Hans Conried.

Color, Not rated, 110m.

This ever-so-light musical stars Garland as a financially strapped farmer who's semi-engaged to fuddy-duddy businessman Bracken. When her flighty sister (De Haven) brings home Kelly and his troupe of actors to rehearse in Garland's barn, she rejects the idea at first, but, of course, she eventually gives in and joins the fun. The Harry Warren/Mack Gordon songs include "You, Wonderful You" and "Get Happy," which was shot three months after the rest of the film with a noticeably thinner Garland. Kelly dances on newspapers. Phil Silvers and Hans Conried are also enjoyable in supporting roles.

THAT'LL BE THE DAY

1973

DIRECTOR: Claude Whatham.

SCREENPLAY: Ray Connolly.

CAST: David Essex, Ringo Starr, Rosemary Leach, James Booth, Billy Fury, Keith Moon, Rosalind Ayres.

Color, PG rated, 90m.

Essex is a working-class kid with nothing but his winning personality to get him where he wants to go, and he wants to go far. He's driven by the desire to be a rock star, and to have the money and excitement that comes with it. Essex is a charismatic actor in his own right, so he's very convincing in his portrayal of this kid with star potential. Essex continues his story in *Stardust* (1974), directed by Michael Apted.

THAT'S ENTERTAINMENT III

1994

DIRECTOR: Bud Friedgen, Michael J. Sheridan.

CAST: Eleanor Powell, Ann Miller, Gene Kelly, Esther Williams, June Allyson.

Color, G rated, 145m.

This third in the series of collected musical numbers from MGM studios was not widely released to theaters and could easily be mistaken for Parts I and II on the video store shelves. It also has the distinction of including musical numbers that were cut from movies before their release and have never been seen before by audiences. So even musical fans will see something new here. Numbers include Lena Horne singing "Ain't It the Truth" and Judy Garland doing "Mr. Monotony." There are several fascinating segments that use a split screen to show two versions of the same number done by different performers. This is a wonderfully entertaining compilation, if not the best of the three, a close second to Part I, which was released more than 20 years ago, in 1974. And if you've missed Parts I and II, now's the time to enjoy them all.

Mystery/Suspense

THE ANDERSON TAPES

1971

DIRECTOR: Sidney Lumet.

SCREENPLAY: Frank R. Pierson, from the novel by Lawrence Sanders.

CAST: Sean Connery, Martin Balsam, Dyan Cannon, Alan King, Ralph Meeker.

Color, PG rated, 98m.

When Connery gets out of prison, he immediately forms a gang to pull off a big job, robbing every tenant in a large New York apartment building. Unfortunately, he's been under surveillance since he left prison, and his phone conversations are being recorded. In fact, every phone in the apartment building has been tapped. Connery heads a great cast in this suspenseful thriller that never lets up. Christopher Walken's film debut.

APARTMENT ZERO

1988

DIRECTOR: Martin Donovan.

SCREENPLAY: Martin Donovan, David Koepp.

CAST: Colin Firth, Hart Bochner, Dora Bryan, Liz Smith.

Color, R rated, 114m.

Firth is a stuffy, meticulous film buff who owns a revival movie theater in Buenos Aires. A native Argentinian, he lives

in an apartment building that caters to English tenants. His theater doesn't bring in much income, so he takes in a charming, ruggedly handsome American boarder with a mysterious past (Bochner). Their relationship becomes increasingly complex, as Firth becomes obsessed with Bochner. This moody, psychological thriller will keep you guessing to its bizarre finale. The soundtrack is very provocative, combining the tango-esque music of Elia Cmiral with intriguing, disquieting sound effects.

THE BEGUILED

1971

DIRECTOR: Don Siegel.

SCREENPLAY: John B. Sherry, Grimes Grice, from the novel by Thomas Cullinan.

CAST: Clint Eastwood, Geraldine Page, Elizabeth Hartman, Jo Ann Harris, Darleen Carr.

Color, R rated, 109m.

There aren't any squinty-eyed shoot-outs in this unusual drama. Released the same year as his *Dirty Harry,* the film stars Eastwood as a wounded Union soldier taken in by the head of a Confederate school for young women. Jealousies soon develop, building to a shocking climax. Good acting, and a dark, foreboding atmosphere are the highlights of this suspenseful drama.

BLOOD SIMPLE

1983

DIRECTOR: Joel Coen.

SCREENPLAY: Joel Coen, Ethan Coen.

CAST: John Getz, Frances McDormand, Dan Hedaya, M. Emmet Walsh.

Color, R rated, 99m.

Bar owner Hedaya hires a private detective to kill his wife and her lover, but things don't work out as he expected. The

detective (Walsh) intends to keep the money and not kill anybody. Set in a small Texas town, this clever little thriller allows the audience in on what's happening, while the characters are left in the dark. Loaded with delectable plot twists, quirky characters and a big dose of black humor, this is a visually dazzling, violent, sometimes hilarious joyride. An impressive debut for brothers Joel and Ethan Coen (*Fargo*).

BLOW OUT

1981

DIRECTOR: Brian De Palma.

SCREENPLAY: Brian De Palma.

CAST: John Travolta, Nancy Allen, John Lithgow, Dennis Franz.

Color, R rated, 107m.

Strangely enough, this strong follow-up to *Dressed to Kill* didn't make a big splash. Travolta is excellent as a movie sound-effects man who becomes embroiled in a murder case (he didn't get another chance to show his stuff until his roaring comeback in *Pulp Fiction*, over a decade later). One of the best conspiracy movies ever made, this taut thriller also features a somewhat perverse interpretation of Hitchcock's fireworks scene in *To Catch a Thief*. Lithgow is effective in an uncharacteristic role as a psychopathic killer. As can be expected in a De Palma movie, the R rating indicates a fair amount of sex, strong language, and violence.

LE BOUCHER aka THE BUTCHER

1969

DIRECTOR: Claude Chabrol.

SCREENPLAY: Claude Chabrol.

CAST: Stéphane Audran, Jean Yanne, Antonio Passalia, Mario Beccaria.

Color, PG rated, 94m. Subtitled.

After a failed love affair, schoolteacher Audran gets involved with the quiet, unassuming butcher (Yanne), in a small French village. When a series of sex murders of young women are committed in the area, a sense of foreboding overcomes her as she comes to the horrifying conclusion that her lover is the murderer. This tense, psychological thriller is beautifully photographed in an idyllic small town, with some nice Hitchcockian touches. Avoid the dubbed version.

THE COMFORT OF STRANGERS

1991

DIRECTOR: Paul Schrader.

SCREENPLAY: Harold Pinter, from the novel by Ian McEwan.

CAST: Chrisopher Walken, Natasha Richardson, Rupert Everett, Helen Mirren.

Color, R rated, 105m.

Christopher Walken is gloriously evil in this film about a young British couple, vacationing in Venice, who are drawn into a relationship with a disturbing stranger. Walken conveys menace like nobody else, and his monologue about his father is worth the price of admission. This dark, unsettling film will pull you under its spell if you let it. The cinematography by Danté Spinotti and the lush score by Angelo Badalamenti help create an atmosphere of claustrophobia and dread mixed with intoxicating beauty.

THE CONVERSATION

1974

DIRECTOR: Francis Ford Coppola.

SCREENPLAY: Francis Ford Coppola.

CAST: Gene Hackman, John Cazale, Allen Garfield, Frederick Forrest, Cindy Williams, Teri Garr, Harrison Ford.

Color, PG rated, 113m.

In this disturbing thriller, an obsessive surveillance expert (Hackman), fearing that the recordings he's making on his latest job will lead to murder, tries to prevent it. Released between his *Godfather,* Parts I and II, this is one of Coppola's best, and certainly one of the great films of the 1970s. Sadly, it didn't get the audience it deserved. Writing, direction, acting (especially by Hackman) and sound (designed by Walter Murch) are all outstanding. It shouldn't be missed. Oscar nominations for Best Picture and Screenplay.

CUTTER'S WAY aka CUTTER AND BONE

1981

DIRECTOR: Ivan Passer.

SCREENPLAY: Jeffrey Alan Fiskin, from the novel by Newton Thornburg.

CAST: Jeff Bridges, John Heard, Lisa Eichhorn, Ann Dusenberry, Stephen Elliott, Nina Van Pallandt.

Color, R rated, 109m.

Heard and Bridges give memorable performances as two unlikely friends. Cutter (Heard) is an embittered, disabled Vietnam veteran, and Bone (Bridges) is an upper-class, womanizing layabout who gets by on his good looks and charm. Together, they get involved in a scheme to extort money from an oil tycoon they suspect of murder, but it soon turns into an obsessive quest for justice. From the opening shots of a festive parade that's out of sync with the music we hear, this unusual thriller has an otherworldly, dreamlike quality. It's a masterful murder mystery with a slam-bang finale. Great score by Jack Nitzsche.

DEFENCE OF THE REALM

1985

DIRECTOR: David Drury.

SCREENPLAY: Martin Stillman.

CAST: Gabriel Byrne, Greta Scacchi, Denholm Elliott, Ian Bannen, Bill Paterson.

Color, PG rated, 96m.

This gripping political thriller is set in contemporary Britain. Hard-bitten journalist Byrne destroys the career of a Labor Party leader (Bannen), only to discover that he'd been set up with bad information by the Tory government. Determined to uncover the sinister conspiracy with the help of seasoned reporter Elliott, he finds that they've both become targets of the powers that be. Byrne and Elliott are both excellent.

EXOTICA

1994

DIRECTOR: Atom Egoyan.

SCREENPLAY: Atom Egoyan.

CAST: Bruce Greenwood, Mia Kirschner, Don McKellar, Elias Koteas, Arsinée Khanjian.

Color, R rated, 104m.

Five lives become intertwined around a strip club called Exotica, in this dark, erotic mystery that won the Canadian Genie Award for Best Canadian Film in 1994. Greenwood is a tax accountant who spends his evenings at the club and always asks to have the girlish Kirschner dance for him at his table. Clues to the relationship between Greenwood and the other four characters are revealed through flashbacks, as the story builds to its surprising conclusion. Challenging and highly original, this sensual mystery is engrossing.

EXPERIMENT IN TERROR

1962

DIRECTOR: Blake Edwards.

SCREENPLAY: The Gordons, from their novel.

CAST: Glenn Ford, Lee Remick, Ross Martin, Stephanie Powers, Ned Glass.

B&W, Not rated, 123m.

Blake Edwards takes you by the throat and doesn't let go in this thriller set in San Francisco. Remick is a bank teller terrorized by an unknown man (Martin), who threatens to kill her and her teenage sister (Powers) if she doesn't help him rob the bank where she works. Against his instructions, she contacts FBI agent Ford. The superbly controlled performances by Remick, Ford, and Martin, the believable plot, and the taut direction by Edwards, make this a satisfying nerve jangler. Fine score by Henry Mancini.

FALLEN IDOL

1948

DIRECTOR: Carol Reed.

SCREENPLAY: Graham Greene, from his story "The Basement Room."

CAST: Ralph Richardson, Michèle Morgan, Bobby Henrey, Sonia Dresdel, Jack Hawkins.

B&W, Not rated, 94m.

Eight-year-old Henrey tries to protect Richardson, the butler he idolizes, when he suspects that Richardson has murdered his hateful wife (Dresdel). But he fears that he knows too much, and may be Richardson's next victim. Told largely from the boy's point of view, this is a sleek, efficient thriller with marvelous tension and great performances, especially by Henrey as the terrified child. Director Reed and screenwriter Greene both received Oscar nominations. They collaborated again, in 1949, on the classic *The Third Man,* and in 1959 on *Our Man in Havana.*

FIVE FINGERS

1952

DIRECTOR: Joseph L. Mankiewiez.

SCREENPLAY: Michael Wilson, from the novel *Operation Cicero* by L. C. Moyzisch.

CAST: James Mason, Danielle Darrieux, Michael Rennie, Walter Hampden.

B&W, Not rated, 108m.

During World War II, the fastidious valet to the British ambassador in Ankara, Turkey decides to get rich by selling Allied secrets to the Nazis. This absorbing, fact-based story reveals the details of his elaborate scheme and the British government's attempts to catch him. Mason is excellent as the amoral Cicero, as the Germans nicknamed him. He never loses his cool as he races to get out of the country with both the British and the Germans in pursuit. The story builds to an exciting climax with some surprising twists. Academy Award nominations went to the director and screenwriter. Score by Bernard Herrmann.

THE FOURTH MAN

1979

DIRECTOR: Paul Verhoeven.

SCREENPLAY: Gerard Soeteman, from the novel by Gerard Reve.

CAST: Jeroen Krabbé, Renee Soutendijk, Thom Hoffman.

Color, Not rated (nudity, violence), 102m. Available subtitled or dubbed.

Krabbé is a heavy-drinking, homosexual writer who has an affair with a beautiful young woman (Soutendijk), with the real intent of meeting her attractive fiancé (Hoffman), who'll soon be returning from a trip. When he learns that Soutendijk has been widowed three times by accidental death, he has hallucinations (or are they premonitions?) that

she intends to murder her fiancé after they're married. Director Verhoeven is having fun with us with this enjoyably off-kilter, erotic thriller. Not released in the U.S. until 1984.

GREEN FOR DANGER

1946

DIRECTOR: Sidney Gilliat.

SCREENPLAY: Sidney Gilliat, Claud Guerney, from the novel by Christianna Brand.

CAST: Alastair Sim, Sally Gray, Rosamund John, Trevor Howard, Leo Genn, Megs Jenkins, Judy Campbell, Ronald Ward.

B&W, Not rated, 93m.

Suspicious deaths in the operating room of a rural English emergency hospital during World War II prompt an investigation from Inspector Cockrill (Sim) of Scotland Yard. The hospital staff gives the nosy intruder the cold shoulder, but the ever diligent Cockrill smells murder in the air and has to sort out the intrigues and rivalries among the staff to find the culprit. Sim leads a stellar cast with his wryly witty performance as the unflappable Inspector Cockrill. A classic whodunit.

GAY TALESE

Mascara (1987), directed by Patrick Conrad.

They Shoot Horses, Don't They? (1969), directed by Sydney Pollack.

Gay Talese has written *Honor Thy Father* and *The Kingdom and the Power.* He lives in New York.

THE GRIFTERS

1990

DIRECTOR: Stephen Frears.

SCREENPLAY: Donald E. Westlake, from the novel by Jim Thompson.

CAST: John Cusack, Anjelica Huston, Annette Bening.

Color, R rated, 114m.

Huston has an aura of steely danger about her in this grim portrait of three con artists and their deadly games. Cusack makes his living doing small-time cons, suckering sailors in card games, or changing $20 bills. Bening uses her beauty and her body, and it's all so easy for her, too. But she wants the two of them to shoot higher, and has an idea of how to do it. When Cusack's mother (Huston) comes back into his life, her ruthless ambitions and jealousy result in tragedy. The three stars are at their best, with Huston outstanding as Cusack's icily amoral mother. The Oscar nominations for Huston, Bening and screenwriter Westlake didn't translate into box office success. Co-produced and narrated by Martin Scorsese.

HIGH AND LOW

1963

DIRECTOR: Akira Kurosawa.

SCREENPLAY: Hideo Oguni, Ryuzo Kikushima, Eifiro Hisaito, Akira Kurosawa, from the novel *The King's Ransom* by Ed McBain.

CAST: Toshiro Mifune, Kyoko Kagawa, Tatsuya Nakadai.

B&W, Not rated, 142m. Subtitled.

Gondo (Mifune) is a wealthy businessman on the verge of making a big deal when he receives a call telling him that his son has been kidnapped. He's ready to forgo his business investment and pay the ransom, when his son turns up, and it becomes clear that the kidnapper has taken the chauffeur's son

by mistake. Gondo's faced with a moral dilemma—should he bankrupt himself paying the ransom because his own son was the target? The first half of this fascinating police drama deals with his agonizing decision. The second half is a fantastically detailed, nuts-and-bolts account of how the police track down the culprit. Just sit back and watch how it's done. A great film.

HOMICIDE

1991

DIRECTOR: David Mamet.

SCREENPLAY: David Mamet.

CAST: Joe Mantegna, William H. Macy, Natalija Nogulich, Ving Rhames, Rebecca Pidgeon, J. J. Johnston, Jack Wallace.

Color, R rated, 102m.

Bobby Gold (Mantegna) is a tough-minded, no-nonsense cop who's in the midst of a case he hopes will lead to a promotion, when he's reassigned to an investigation of the murder of an old Jewish shopkeeper. Her family thinks it's a hate crime, not a robbery attempt. As he reluctantly digs deeper into the case, he's also forced to deal with his own unacknowledged Jewish ties. Mantegna gives a solid performance as the hard-boiled cop. He's worked often with Mamet, and he's well-suited to his style. Mamet's crisp, authentic dialogue is a pleasure to hear. A tough, suspenseful film.

HOPSCOTCH

1980

DIRECTOR: Ronald Neame.

SCREENPLAY: Brian Garfield, Bryan Forbes, from the novel by Brian Garfield.

CAST: Walter Matthau, Glenda Jackson, Ned Beatty, Sam Waterston, Herbert Lom, George Baker.

Color, R rated, 104m.

This lighthearted romp stars Matthau as a CIA operative who takes revenge on his idiot boss, Beatty, by threatening to publish his memoirs. Waterston, his ex-partner, is assigned to find him, and stop him. Matthau leads them on a merry chase, always anticipating their next move, mocking them by setting traps. This fast-paced spy-comedy-chase combo has lots of action and some hilarious bits. Matthau and Jackson, as his willing accomplice, are teamed up here again after the success of *House Calls* (1978).

HOUSE OF GAMES

1987

DIRECTOR: David Mamet.

SCREENPLAY: David Mamet.

CAST: Lindsay Crouse, Joe Mantegna, Mike Nussbaum, Lilia Skala.

Color, R rated, 102m.

Psychiatrist Crouse seeks out con man Mantegna when a compulsive gambler she's treating reveals that he owes Mantegna a lot of money. But instead of getting her patient out of his jam, she becomes intrigued by the scams that Mantegna's gang pulls, and becomes involved. In his first time out as a director, Mamet gives us a sophisticated, psychological thriller that keeps us guessing. The complex plot offers up some shocks and a good deal of laughter. Crouse was Mamet's wife at the time.

I CONFESS

1953

DIRECTOR: Alfred Hitchcock.

SCREENPLAY: George Tabori, William Archibald, from the play by Paul Anthelme.

CAST: Montgomery Clift, Karl Malden, Anne Baxter, Brian Aherne.

B&W, Not rated, 95m.

This brooding drama, filmed in Quebec, stars Clift as a dedicated young priest who hears the confession of a man who's committed a murder, but bound by the sanctity of the confessional, can't tell the police what he knows. When the police discover that the murdered man was blackmailing Clift about a love affair he'd had with Baxter before he became a priest, he's charged with the murder. Clift gives a controlled performance as the doomed priest, and the film has a strikingly ominous atmosphere. The haunting vocals of Dimitri Tiomkin's score add a mystical quality. Although considered a "lesser" Hitchcock, it delivers a compelling story that builds to an exciting and satisfying climax.

IN A LONELY PLACE

1950

DIRECTOR: Nicholas Ray.

SCREENPLAY: Andrew Solt, from a novel by Dorothy B. Hughes.

CAST: Humphrey Bogart, Gloria Grahame, Frank Lovejoy, Robert Warwick.

B&W, Not rated, 91m.

Bogart is Dixon Steele, a screenwriter who hasn't had a hit in years, and when a young woman who was seen with him turns up dead, he becomes a suspect. His girlfriend, Grahame, wants to believe in his innocence, but unfortunately, Bogart has a short fuse, and she's been the victim of his violent temper. Bogart's performance as the troubled writer, and the cynical, sharp dialogue by Solt give this suspenseful psychological drama its punch. Ray's direction is straightforward and efficient. Grahame and Ray were married when this was filmed. They were soon divorced.

KNIFE IN THE HEAD

1978

DIRECTOR: Reinhard Hauff.

SCREENPLAY: Peter Schneider.

CAST: Bruno Ganz, Angela Winkler, Heinz Hönig, Hans Brenner, Hans Christian Blech.

Color, Not rated (profanity, nudity, sexual situations), 108m. Subtitled.

Biogeneticist Ganz, shot in the head during a police raid, is left partially paralyzed, with memory loss and speech impairment. As he lies helpless in his hospital bed, the police attempt to frame him for attempted murder, and he becomes a pawn between the police and a terrorist organization. The suspense builds as the police, believing him to be faking his symptoms, attempt to move him to a prison hospital, cutting him off from his friends. Ganz brilliantly conveys the vulnerability and isolation of this man who can't speak for himself, in this absorbing psychological thriller.

THE LATE SHOW

1977

DIRECTOR: Robert Benton.

SCREENPLAY: Robert Benton.

CAST: Art Carney, Lily Tomlin, Bill Macy, Eugene Roche, Joanna Cassidy, Howard Duff.

Color, PG rated, 94m.

Ira Wells (Carney) is a crusty, world-weary private eye with a bad stomach and a hearing aid, whose ex-partner has just been murdered while looking for kooky Tomlin's missing cat. But enough about the plot. The chemistry between Carney and Tomlin is what makes this little comedy-mystery percolate, and Macy and Roche are good in supporting parts. It makes you wish they'd do a sequel. Benton got an Oscar nomination for his screenplay. Produced by Robert Altman.

THE LAUGHING POLICEMAN

1973

DIRECTOR: Stuart Rosenberg.

SCREENPLAY: Thomas Rickman, from the novel by Per Wahloo and Maj Sjowall.

CAST: Walter Matthau, Bruce Dern, Lou Gossett, Jr., Albert Paulsen, Anthony Zerbe.

Color, R rated, 111m.

Don't be misled by the title. This is a gritty, violent police thriller. Matthau plays Jake Martin, a veteran San Francisco detective whose partner is killed when a maniac massacres the passengers on a bus. A tired, despondent Matthau works with his new partner, Dern, on the case, which is complicated by copycat attacks. The urgency builds as they try to find the killer before he strikes again. Gripping suspense, presented in a realistic, unsentimental, semidocumentary style.

LAWRENCE BLOCK

Alice Doesn't Live Here Anymore (1974), directed by Martin Scorsese.

Payday (1972), directed by Daryl Duke.

Same Time Next Year (1978), directed by Robert Mulligan.

Tender Mercies (1983), directed by Bruce Beresford.

The April Fools (1969), directed by Stuart Rosenberg.

Lawrence Block, a Mystery Writers of America Grand Master, is most recently the author of *A Long Line of Dead Men* and *The Burglar Who Thought He Was Bogart.* He would just as soon not talk about the three films made of his novels. He lives in Greenwich Village.

THE LONG GOODBYE

1973

DIRECTOR: Robert Altman.

SCREENPLAY: Leigh Brackett, from the novel by Raymond Chandler.

CAST: Elliott Gould, Nina van Pallandt, Sterling Hayden, Mark Rydell, Henry Gibson, Jim Bouton.

Color, R rated, 112m.

Altman's revisionist version of the Chandler classic brought howls of outrage from fans when it was released. As played by Gould, in perhaps his best performance, Philip Marlowe is a laid-back, bemused fellow whose favorite expression is "It's OK with me." He's not exactly a ball of fire. Hayden and Gibson provide great, campy performances in supporting roles. Even John Williams's score is a joke, as he provides endless, imaginative variations on the title song. Just take it on its own terms and enjoy the ride. The ending is a shocker.

MIRAGE

1965

DIRECTOR: Edward Dmytryk.

SCREENPLAY: Peter Stone.

CAST: Gregory Peck, Diane Baker, Kevin McCarthy, Jack Weston, George Kennedy, Walter Matthau.

B&W, Not rated, 109m.

David Stillwell (Peck) has lost his memory during a power outage in the building where he works. Everyone seems out to confuse him, and he's being chased by men with guns. He hires Matthau, a private detective, to find out who he is, and why these people are after him. The trouble is, it's Matthau's first case. There's an effective feeling of disorientation in this intricately plotted, Hitchcockian thriller, as Peck gamely tries

to piece the puzzle of his life back together. Matthau steals every scene he's in as the droll novice detective.

MONSIEUR HIRE

1989

DIRECTOR: Patrice Le Conte.

SCREENPLAY: Patrice Le Conte, Patrick Dewolf, from a novel by Georges Simenon.

CAST: Michel Blanc, Sandrine Bonnaire, André Wilms, Luc Thuillier.

Color, PG-13 rated, 82m. Subtitled.

A lonely, middle-aged man (Blanc), disliked by his neighbors, becomes the prime suspect in the murder of a neighborhood girl. There isn't enough evidence to arrest him, but he continues to be hounded by the detective on the case (Wilms). A beautiful young woman (Bonnaire) who lives across the alley notices that he's been watching her from his window, and introduces herself. As the story unfolds, Blanc's subtle performance creates empathy with this man, and the motives of the seductive Bonnaire come into question. This precisely made and intriguing film has an erotic undercurrent that adds to the tension as it plays a cat-and-mouse game with the audience's emotions. The effectively moody score is by Michael Nyman.

MURDER AT THE GALLOP

1963

DIRECTOR: George Pollock.

SCREENPLAY: James P. Cavanagh, from *After the Funeral* by Agatha Christie.

CAST: Margaret Rutherford, Robert Morley, Flora Robson, Stringer Davis, Charles Tingwell.

B&W, Not rated, 82m.

Miss Marple investigates the death of a wealthy old man who was scared to death by a cat, or so it seems. She and her assistant, Mr. Stringer (her real-life husband, Stringer Davis), make the rounds, peering into windows and pestering the police. There's a lot to be suspicious about when it comes to the old man's heirs, and none of them is safe. Morley and Rutherford are hysterical in their scenes together. This is probably the best of the Miss Marple series featuring Margaret Rutherford.

THE NARROW MARGIN

1952

DIRECTOR:	Richard Fleischer.
SCREENPLAY:	Earl Fenton.
CAST:	Charles McGraw, Marie Windsor, Jacqueline White, Queenie Leonard.

B&W, Not rated, 70m.

Tough cop McGraw must safely transport a gangster's widow by train from Chicago to L.A. to testify before a grand jury. Pursued by hit men who don't know what she looks like, McGraw has to keep her whereabouts on the train secret. Well-paced action, with a masterful use of the enclosed, high-speed train setting by the director, keeps the tension high. Oscar-nominated for its original story by Martin Goldsmith and Jack Leonard, the film was made for under $200,000. The 1990 remake with Gene Hackman couldn't top the original.

NIGHT MOVES

1975

DIRECTOR:	Arthur Penn.
SCREENPLAY:	Alan Sharp.
CAST:	Gene Hackman, Jennifer Warren, Susan Clark, Edward Binns, Melanie Griffith, Kenneth Mars.

Color, R rated, 95m.

Director Penn is in a somber mood in this underrated detective story. Hackman is an L.A. private eye whose wife (Clark) is having an affair, so he takes a job looking for runaway teenager Griffith, who's fled to the Florida Keys. The movie has a dark, melancholy atmosphere that matches Hackman's beaten-down detective's view of the world. Builds to a slam-bang finale.

NIGHT OF THE HUNTER

1955

DIRECTOR: Charles Laughton.

SCREENPLAY: James Agee, from a novel by Davis Grubb.

CAST: Robert Mitchum, Shelley Winters, Lillian Gish, Don Beddoe, Evelyn Varden, Peter Graves, James Gleason.

B&W, Not rated, 93m.

This unusual combination of lyrical fantasy and chilling horror flopped at the box office, and Laughton's first film as director became his only one. Malevolent "soul-saver" Mitchum, in perhaps his best performance, is the scariest preacher you'll ever see. He marries timorous Shelley Winters, and that's bad news for her children, because they know the location of the money stolen by their father before his death, and Mitchum wants it. The children run away in terror, and Mitchum tracks them across the countryside to kindly old lady Gish's house, where he finds a formidable opponent. Visually stunning and truly frightening, this is a movie you won't soon forget. Score by Walter Schumann.

OBSESSION

1976

DIRECTOR: Brian De Palma.

SCREENPLAY: Paul Schrader.

CAST: Cliff Robertson, Genevieve Bujold, John Lithgow, Sylvia Williams, Wanda Blackman, Patrick McNamara.

Color, PG rated, 98m.

Widower Robertson feels responsible when his wife and child are killed during a kidnapping attempt, and he gives his life over to guilt. When he sees a woman who seems the double of his dead wife while on a trip to Italy, he become obsessed with her and convinces her to return to New Orleans with him. This visually stunning, moody homage to Hitchcock stands on its own, but was vastly underrated upon its release because of the critics' fixation on comparing it to *Vertigo*. The Oscar-nominated score by Bernard Herrmann enhances the film's mesmerizing quality.

ODD MAN OUT

1947

DIRECTOR: Carol Reed.

SCREENPLAY: F. L. Green, R. C. Sherriff.

CAST: James Mason, Robert Newton, Cyril Cusack, Kathleen Ryan, Robert Beatty.

B&W, Not rated, 111m.

Mason is an Irish rebel, recently released from prison, who is wounded during a payroll holdup. Separated from his accomplices, he becomes the subject of a manhunt through the streets of Belfast, as he's losing blood. The people he meets are afraid to help him, but they don't want to turn him in, either. At one point, he's taken by a drunken artist (Newton) to his studio in an abandoned building, because he wants to paint the portrait of a dying man. The stark night scenes evoke feelings of loneliness and helplessness as Mason wanders through the streets, losing strength. Mason is exceptional in what he called his best movie role. Gripping drama.

OUT OF THE PAST

1947

DIRECTOR: Jacques Tourneur.

SCREENPLAY: Geoffrey Homes, from his novel *Build My Gallows High.*

CAST: Robert Mitchum, Jane Greer, Kirk Douglas, Rhonda Fleming, Richard Webb.

B&W, Not rated, 97m.

Retired private eye Mitchum, living peacefully in a small California town, finds himself drawn back into his former, shady life, in this film noir classic. Through flashbacks, Mitchum tells his girlfriend (Fleming) about his past dealings with slimy gangster Douglas, and the job he took finding Douglas's girlfriend (Greer), who'd taken off with $40,000 of his money. Mitchum is super in this early starring role, and Douglas is appropriately despicable in this moody thriller, shot in high-contrast style by cinematographer Nicholas Musuraca. Remade in 1984 as *Against All Odds.*

THE PLUMBER

1980

DIRECTOR: Peter Weir.

SCREENPLAY: Peter Weir.

CAST: Judy Morris, Ivan Kants, Robert Coleby, Candy Raymond.

Color, Not rated, 76m.

An affable plumber named Max (Kants) appears at the door of a couple's apartment unbidden to "check the pipes," and proceeds to tear the bathroom apart. Morris, an anthropologist whose husband is at work at the university, becomes increasingly uncomfortable with Max's overly familiar demeanor, which becomes intimidating. As the job drags out over several days, she's filled with dread in anticipation of his return, but she can't explain her intense reaction to her bemused husband. Weir does a great job of creating an

atmosphere of apprehension in a normal, everyday setting, and Kants is very good as the unsettling workman. An unusual psychological thriller with a good dose of black humor. Made for Australian TV.

RIFIFI

1955

DIRECTOR: Jules Dassin.

SCREENPLAY: René Wheeler, Jules Dassin, Auguste LeBreton, from the novel by LeBreton.

CAST: Jean Servais, Carl Mohner, Robert Manuel, Marie Sabouret, Perlo Vita (Jules Dassin).

B&W, Not rated, 116m. Subtitled or dubbed.

This French heist movie set the standard for all that were to follow, including the director's own *Topkapi.* It opens with twenty minutes of silence, as we watch a gang of thieves work meticulously to dismantle the security system and open the safe in a jewelry store. We're drawn in as we watch what they're doing, and it puts us on their side, hoping that nothing goes wrong. The surprise is that after working so well together in the burglary, they turn against each other with tragic results. Director Dassin, an American, moved to Europe in the 1950s after being blacklisted, and he made his best-known films there.

ROAD HOUSE

1948

DIRECTOR: Jean Negulesco.

SCREENPLAY: Edward Chodorov.

CAST: Ida Lupino, Cornel Wilde, Richard Widmark, Celeste Holm.

B&W, Not rated, 95m.

Jefty (Widmark) owns a roadhouse, and Wilde, his best friend, is his manager. Jefty returns from a trip to Chicago with sultry singer Lupino. He has more than music in mind

with Lupino, but she's interested in Wilde. When Jefty finds out, he turns into a jealous whacko and frames Wilde for a burglary. Great-looking, moody atmosphere with good suspense that leads to a knockout finale. Lupino introduces the song "Again" in a seductively husky voice.

SABOTAGE

1936

DIRECTOR: Alfred Hitchcock.

SCREENPLAY: Charles Bennett, Ian Hay, Helen Simpson, E. V. H. Emmett, from the novel *The Secret Agent* by Joseph Conrad.

CAST: Oscar Homolka, Sylvia Sidney, John Loder, Desmond Tester, Joyce Barbour, Matthew Boulton.

B&W, Not rated, 76m.

The Verlocs (Sidney and Homolka) are a married couple who run a small London movie theater. Unknown to his wife, the unassuming Mr. Verloc is a dangerous secret agent. But when her younger brother (Tester) is killed in a bus explosion while delivering a package for her husband, Mrs. Verloc begins to suspect that he may be responsible. Hitchcock makes great use of shadow to create the dark mood in this crafty thriller, and he demonstrates some of the techniques that he'll use in his later classics. This may be the best of his English features, but it didn't do well at the box office.

SCREAM OF FEAR aka TASTE OF FEAR

1961

DIRECTOR: Seth Holt.

SCREENPLAY: Jimmy Sangster.

CAST: Susan Strasberg, Ann Todd, Ronald Lewis, Christopher Lee, Leonard Sachs.

B&W, Not rated, 82m.

Shocks and frights are the mainstay of this suspenseful little thriller from England. Strasberg is a young, crippled woman who is heir to her father's large fortune. Having not seen him in many years, she goes to the Riviera to visit him, only to be told by her stepmother that he's away on business. But Strasberg thinks she's seen his corpse. The plot, borrowed from *Diabolique,* is filled with little tricks and deceptions to keep the audience guessing.

SEANCE ON A WET AFTERNOON

1964

DIRECTOR: Bryan Forbes.

SCREENPLAY: Bryan Forbes, from the novel by Mark McShane.

CAST: Kim Stanley, Richard Attenborough, Nanette Newman, Patrick Magee.

B&W, Not rated, 121m.

Stanley is a loony, phony medium who coerces her servile husband (Attenborough) into kidnapping a young boy so she can later reveal his location, making a name for herself. When her scheme falls apart, Attenborough must bear the consequences with her. Stanley was nominated for an Oscar for her extravagant performance as the demented medium. A relentless chiller.

SEE NO EVIL

1971

DIRECTOR: Richard Fleischer.

SCREENPLAY: Brian Clemens.

CAST: Mia Farrow, Dorothy Alison, Lila Kaye, Diane Grayson.

Color, PG rated, 89m.

This English thriller takes right off as we see the boots of an unidentified man walking down the road, accompanied by the rousing opening music by Elmer Bernstein. We next see

Farrow, a young woman recently blinded by a fall from her horse, as she returns home from the hospital to her family's country estate. She's still getting adjusted to her new condition, when she discovers the bodies of her family in different parts of the house. The shock of that moment sets the tone for the rest of the movie as she desperately tries to escape. A real nail-biter.

SHADOW OF A DOUBT

1943

DIRECTOR: Alfred Hitchcock.

SCREENPLAY: Thornton Wilder, Sally Benson, Alma Reville, from a story by Gordon McDonnell.

CAST: Joseph Cotten, Teresa Wright, Hume Cronyn, Macdonald Carey, Patricia Collinge, Henry Travers, Wallace Ford.

B&W, Not rated, 108m.

When suave Uncle Charlie (Cotten) comes to visit his sister's all-American family in idyllic Santa Rosa, California, his teenage niece (Wright), who idolizes him, couldn't be happier. But Charlie, who's her favorite uncle's namesake, is the only one who learns the truth about his dark and sinister past. Cotten is brilliant as the charming Uncle Charlie, and Hume Cronyn is hilarious as the neighbor who's fixated on how to commit the perfect murder. This quietly disturbing Hitchcock classic isn't as widely seen as many of his films, but this dark slice of Americana is said to be one of Hitchcock's own favorites.

SHALLOW GRAVE

1994

DIRECTOR: Danny Boyle.

SCREENPLAY: John Hodge.

CAST: Kerry Fox, Christopher Eccleston, Ewan McGregor.

Color, R rated, 94m.

Three Edinburgh roommates, two men and a woman, take in a fourth, only to find him dead in his room next to a suitcase full of cash. After they decide to keep the money and bury the body in the woods, they're feeling pretty pleased with themselves, until they start worrying about where the money came from, and whether they can trust each other. Full of surprises, this stylish and energetic directing debut is dripping with venomous humor, and blood.

A SHOCK TO THE SYSTEM

1990

DIRECTOR:	Jan Egleson.
SCREENPLAY:	Andrew Klavan, from a novel by Simon Brett.
CAST:	Michael Caine, Elizabeth McGovern, Peter Riegert, Swoozie Kurtz, Will Patton.

Color, R rated, 91m.

After being passed over for promotion, marketing executive Caine starts bumping off his competition, making it look like accidents. He gets the idea after he accidentally pushes a bum under a subway train and realizes how easy it is. His first victim, for practice, is his shrewish wife, Kurtz. Next is Riegert, the guy who got the promotion instead of him. With the success of each murder, he becomes more self-confident and contented. Caine is wickedly funny as the efficient and remorseless murderer, in this gallows humor-thriller. Riegert and Kurtz are good in supporting parts. Interesting score by Gary Chang.

A SOLDIER'S STORY

1984

DIRECTOR:	Norman Jewison.
SCREENPLAY:	Charles Fuller, from his play.

CAST: Howard E. Rollins Jr., Adolph Caesar, Art Evans, David Alan Grier, David Harris, Denzel Washington.

Color, R rated, 101m.

When a black drill sergeant (Caesar) is murdered on a Louisiana army base during World War II, Captain Davenport (Rollins), a black lawyer, is sent by Washington to investigate. When he arrives, he finds that no one wants to talk to him, making his investigation all the more difficult. The details of the crime are shown in flashbacks, as the captain puts the story together. A good study of racial and military attitudes wrapped in an intriguing murder mystery with plenty of twists. Fine performances by Rollins, Washington, and Caesar, who received an Oscar nomination for Supporting Actor. Nominations also as Best Picture and Adapted Screenplay.

THE SPIRAL STAIRCASE

1946

DIRECTOR: Robert Siodmak.

SCREENPLAY: Mel Dinelli, from the novel *Some Must Watch* by Ethel Lina White.

CAST: Dorothy McGuire, George Brent, Kent Smith, Ethel Barrymore, Rhys Williams, Rhonda Fleming.

B&W, Not rated, 83m.

It was a dark and stormy night in a small New England town in 1906. McGuire is a young mute woman who cares for the cantankerous old Barrymore. There have been several murders of young women in the area, and all the victims had some physical flaw. Complete with mysterious footsteps, blowing drapes, slamming doors, and shadows, this is *the* classic "mad strangler on the loose in the old dark house" story.

THE STRANGER ON THE THIRD FLOOR

1940

DIRECTOR: Boris Ingster.

SCREENPLAY: Frank Partos.

CAST: Peter Lorre, John McGuire, Margaret Tallichet, Elisha Cook, Jr., Charles Waldron.

B&W, Not rated, 64m.

In this fast-paced mystery, reputed to be the first film noir, a reporter (McGuire) realizes that his testimony in a murder trial helped convict an innocent man. While he's figuring out what to do about it, he becomes a suspect in the murder of his crotchety neighbor. Lorre has a brief but memorable appearance as the mysterious stranger in the long white scarf, but it's McGuire's wildly paranoid nightmare sequence that is the surprising highlight of this neat little thriller. Art director Van Nest Polglase's next job was on *Citizen Kane.*

STRAY DOG

1949

DIRECTOR: Akira Kurosawa.

SCREENPLAY: Akira Kurosawa, Ryuzo Kikushima.

CAST: Toshiro Mifune, Takashi Shimura, Keiko Awaji.

B&W, Not rated, 122m. Subtitled.

The opening shot is a close-up of a panting dog on the hottest day of the year, and on a crowded bus a policeman (Mifune) has his gun stolen. After discovering that his stolen weapon has been used in a murder, he goes in pursuit of the culprit and his gun through the streets of war-ravaged Tokyo. The oppressive heat and constant downpours add to the misery as he combs the underworld of the city. This tense noirish thriller owes its style to American crime novels, but the story was inspired by a real incident that Kurosawa heard of, involving a Tokyo detective who was unfortunate enough to

lose his pistol during a time immediately after World War II, when there was a shortage of guns.

A STUDY IN TERROR

1965

DIRECTOR: James Hill.

SCREENPLAY: Donald Ford, Derek Ford, from a novel by Ellery Queen.

CAST: John Neville, Donald Houston, John Fraser, Robert Morley, Cecil Parker, Anthony Quayle, Barbara Windsor.

Color, Not rated, 95m.

Sherlock Holmes (Neville) and Dr. Watson (Houston) go after Jack the Ripper and identify who he is, in this violent, well-acted thriller. Houston may be the best Watson, ever. Colorful sets and good period feel. Directed by Academy Award-winning documentary filmmaker James Hill, who also directed *Born Free*.

SUDDENLY

1954

DIRECTOR: Lewis Allen.

SCREENPLAY: Richard Sale.

CAST: Frank Sinatra, Sterling Hayden, James Gleason, Nancy Gates, Kim Charney.

B&W, Not rated, 75m.

This suspense-drama features a surprising performance by Sinatra as the nasty leader of a gang of hired killers who plot to assassinate the President. The dread builds as the family whose home the assassins have taken over as their headquarters attempts to thwart their murderous plans. Released the year after Sinatra's Oscar-winning performance in *From Here to Eternity, Suddenly* is a fine thriller. ("Suddenly" is the name of the town where the action takes place.)

THE TAKING OF PELHAM ONE, TWO, THREE

1974

DIRECTOR: Joseph Sargent.

SCREENPLAY: Peter Stone, from the novel by John Godey.

CAST: Robert Shaw, Walter Matthau, Martin Balsam, Hector Elizondo, Earl Hindman, James Broderick.

Color, R rated, 104m.

Shaw is the ruthless leader of a gang of criminals who highjack a New York subway train, armed with very big guns. The methodical Shaw has planned well, and they quickly go through the motions of securing the train and announcing their ransom demands. Matthau is the head of subway security who's forced to deal with Shaw's demands. Matthau is excellent, as usual, and Shaw is thoroughly convincing as the the cold-blooded ringleader. The tension stays high throughout this gritty, fast-paced thriller.

TO CATCH A KILLER

1991

DIRECTOR: Eric Till.

SCREENPLAY: Jud Kinberg.

CAST: Brian Dennehy, Michael Riley, Margot Kidder, David Eisner.

Color, Not rated, 95m.

This is a taut study of how the police built a case against John Wayne Gacy, a building contractor and seemingly nice guy who murdered 32 young men and boys in a suburb of Chicago. Riley plays the tenacious local cop who persisted in gathering evidence against the arrogant killer, even as he flaunted his disrespect for the police. Dennehy gives a superior performance as Gacy in this engrossing police drama and portrait of evil. Edited from a TV miniseries.

LUCIAN K. TRUSCOTT IV

Thunder Road (1958), directed by Arthur Ripley. The classic moonshine movie starring Robert Mitchum.

White Lightning (1973), directed by Joseph Sargent. The first of Burt Reynolds's *Gator* pictures, to which even Andrew Sarris in the *Voice* gave a rave review as the best "B" picture of the year.

Pat Garrett and Billy the Kid (1973), directed by Sam Peckinpah with Kris Kristofferson and Bob Dylan. The soundtrack by Dylan alone makes the picture worth watching.

The Last Picture Show (1971), directed by Peter Bogdanovich.

Lucian K. Truscott IV wrote the novels *Dress Gray* and *Army Blue.* He lives in Los Angeles.

TOPKAPI

1964

DIRECTOR: Jules Dassin.

SCREENPLAY: Monja Danischewsky, from the Eric Ambler novel *The Light of Day.*

CAST: Peter Ustinov, Robert Morley, Melina Mercouri, Maximilian Schell, Akim Tamiroff.

Color, Not rated, 120m.

Ustinov is an oafish trinket vendor who is hired to drive a car, loaded with contraband, across the border to Istanbul. Once there, he's taken in as a member of a gang that's going to steal jewels from the Topkapi museum. The jewel heist at

the end of the film is done in the style that Dassin established in *Rififi*. Ustinov won a Supporting Actor Oscar for his role as the bumbling, small-time hustler who describes himself as "a carbuncle on the behind of humanity." He steals the movie. Highly entertaining, good-natured fun. The sparkling score is by Manos Hadjidakis.

THE VANISHING

1988

DIRECTOR: George Sluizer.

SCREENPLAY: Tim Krabbé, from his novel *The Golden Egg*.

CAST: Bernard-Pierre Donnadieu, Gene Bervoets, Johanna Ter Steege.

Color, Not rated (violence), 106m. Subtitled.

A happily married science teacher perfects a plan to kidnap an ususpecting young woman. A young Dutch couple, driving through France on vacation, stops at a gas station. The young woman (Ter Steege) goes in alone to fetch drinks, and never returns. The young man (Bervoets) searches obsessively for her for three years, to no avail. As the parallel stories of these two men and their obsessions unfold, this intelligent suspense-thriller builds to a horrifying climax. Brilliantly done. Unsuccessfully remade with Jeff Bridges in 1993.

THE VELVET TOUCH

1948

DIRECTOR: John Gage.

SCREENPLAY: Leo Rosten.

CAST: Rosalind Russell, Leo Genn, Sidney Greenstreet, Claire Trevor, Leon Ames, Frank McHugh.

B&W, Not rated, 97m.

Russell is Valerie Stanton, a famous stage actress who murders her producer (Genn), a blackmailer, in a rage. The story

of their troubled relationship is shown through flashbacks. The police don't suspect her, and it looks like it may have been a perfect crime. Remorseful, she can't see the point in confessing. But can she live a normal life, knowing what she's done? Russell gives a strong performance, and Sidney Greenstreet is great as the police captain who investigates. A well-done psychological mystery.

WHISTLE BLOWER

1986

DIRECTOR: Simon Langton.

SCREENPLAY: Julian Bond, from the novel by John Hale.

CAST: Michael Caine, James Fox, Nigel Havers, Felicity Dean, John Gielgud, Gordon Jackson, Barry Foster.

Color, R rated, 100m.

Michael Caine is a grieving father who believes his bureaucrat son's apparent suicide is really murder, and decides to investigate himself. A former intelligence agent, Caine finds out that his son, a government translator, had uncovered something nasty and had planned to tell a journalist about it before he died. He sets out to find the truth. Caine heads an expert cast with his accomplished, restrained performance, and Gielgud is, as always, dandy in a small role. A skillful political thriller.

THE WINDOW

1949

DIRECTOR: Ted Tetzlaff.

SCREENPLAY: Mel Dinelli, from a story by Cornell Woolrich.

CAST: Bobby Driscoll, Barbara Hale, Arthur Kennedy, Paul Stewart, Ruth Roman.

B&W, Not rated, 73m.

Tommy (Driscoll) is always telling fantastic stories to anyone who'll listen, so when he says he's witnessed a murder through the window of the upstairs apartment, his parents don't believe him. In fact, no one believes him, except the murderer, who decides to shut Tommy up. A pulse-pounding chase through an old abandoned building is the climax of this top-notch thriller. Driscoll won an Oscar as Outstanding Juvenile Actor for his performance.

WOMAN IN THE DUNES

1964

DIRECTOR: Hiroshi Teshigahara.

SCREENPLAY: Kobo Abe.

CAST: Eiji Okada, Kyoto Koshoda.

B&W, Not rated (nudity, sexual situations) 127m. Subtitled.

A young man collecting bugs in the sand dunes misses his bus and is invited by villagers to stay with a local woman who lives at the bottom of an enormous sandpit. The only way in and out is a rope ladder. Everything in her dilapidated shack is covered with the sand that sifts through the roof, and the heat is stifling. When he tries to leave in the morning, he discovers that he's a prisoner, and he's forced into a monotonous routine of digging sand out of the pit for the villagers. This is a stunning psychological thriller that is unforgettable. Hypnotic cinematography by Hiroshi Segawa and music by Tohru Takemitsu.

THE WRONG MAN

1957

DIRECTOR: Alfred Hitchcock.

SCREENPLAY: Maxwell Anderson, Angus MacPhail.

CAST: Henry Fonda, Vera Miles, Anthony Quayle, Harold J. Stone.

B&W, Not rated, 105m.

When musician Fonda is mistakenly identified by witnesses as a robber, his quiet, respectable life is turned upside down. He's arrested, tried and convicted of a crime he didn't commit. After his arrest, his wife collapses under the pressure and has a mental breakdown. Considered to be a departure for Hitchcock, this compelling drama has many of his trademark elements: guilt, dread of authority figures and the police, and an innocent man in peril. Based on the true story of Christopher Emmanuel Valestrero, a New York musician, who was falsely convicted of several robberies before the real culprit was arrested.

Westerns

BAD COMPANY

1972

DIRECTOR: Robert Benton.

SCREENPLAY: David Newman, Robert Benton.

CAST: Jeff Bridges, Barry Brown, Jim Davis, David Huddleston, John Savage.

Color, PG (strong violence), 93m.

Barry Brown, trying hard to avoid conscription into the Army during the Civil War, leaves home to make his escape. He meets Bridges, the leader of a gang of boys who live off thieving and any con they can think of. They decide to head west together to find their fortune. Soon they're half-starved and stealing again. The people they meet are callous and rough-hewn, not so willing to forgive and forget. Life becomes dangerous. This is a tough, unsentimental recreation of the time and place, with good performances, especially by Bridges, and a measured dose of black humor. The muted Gordon Willis cinematography adds to the atmosphere, as does the piano score by Harvey Schmidt. Note that the rating for this film today would be R.

BAD DAY AT BLACK ROCK

1955

DIRECTOR: John Sturges.

SCREENPLAY: Millard Kaufman, from the story "Bad Time at Hondo" by Howard Breslin.

CAST: Spencer Tracy, Robert Ryan, Dean Jagger, Walter Brennan, Ernest Borgnine, Lee Marvin, Anne Francis.

Color, Not rated, 81m.

A one-armed stranger (Tracy) gets off the train at a sleepy desert hamlet, and is greeted by hostility by the townsfolk, who have something to hide. Set in a mythical western town, the action in this contemporary Western, set in 1945, takes place over a twenty-four-hour period. Tracy is John J. McReedy, a war veteran, who's come looking for a Japanese tenant farmer. After he unwittingly discovers the town's ugly secret, the story moves to a violent climax. This is gripping drama, masterfully directed by Sturges, with outstanding performances, especially from Tracy, who received an Oscar nomination, and Ryan, who is convincingly vile. This important film also received nominations for Sturges and the screenplay.

THE BALLAD OF LITTLE JO

1993

DIRECTOR: Maggie Greenwald.

SCREENPLAY: Maggie Greenwald.

CAST: Suzy Amis, Bo Hopkins, Ian McKellen, David Chung, Carrie Snodgress, Rene Auberjonois.

Color, R rated, 120m.

In the 1860s, a young woman (Amis) is forced to give up an illegitimate child and takes off west to start a new life. She quickly learns that it's no place for a woman alone, after narrowly escaping an attempted rape. She gives herself a disfiguring scar, and masquerades as a man for the rest of her life, eventually homesteading her own ranch. This is a rich and involving story, based on a real woman's experiences. Amis is superb as the gutsy young woman, and the supporting cast is excellent as well. David Mansfield composed and performs the music.

BITE THE BULLET

1975

DIRECTOR:	Richard Brooks.
SCREENPLAY:	Richard Brooks.
CAST:	Gene Hackman, James Coburn, Candice Bergen, Ben Johnson, Ian Bannen, Jan-Michael Vincent, Sally Kirkland, Dabney Coleman.

Color, PG rated, 131m.

The horses are the stars of this Western-adventure about a grueling 600-mile horse race across the southwest. In fact, the plight of the horses during the race looks so grim, the makers of the film were quick to reassure the audience that the animals weren't mistreated during production. As to the human characters, Hackman leads the cast of disparate contestants in the torturous endurance test, with Ben Johnson outstanding in support. Intelligent adventure with magnificent scenery photographed by Harry Stradling, Jr. Score by Alex North.

BLOOD ON THE MOON

1948

DIRECTOR:	Robert Wise.
SCREENPLAY:	Lillie Hayward, from a novel by Luke Short.
CAST:	Robert Mitchum, Barbara Bel Geddes, Robert Preston, Walter Brennan, Tom Tully.

B&W, Not rated, 88m.

Drifter Mitchum is summoned by old friend Preston to take a job as a hired gun in a range war. It isn't until he starts working for Preston that he realizes he's on the wrong side, and that his old pal is a ruthless killer. Mitchum and Preston are both convincing as the friends who become enemies, and Brennan and Bel Geddes are perfect as Preston's intended victims. Lots of convincing action that leads inexorably to a big shootout finale. A classic Western.

DUEL AT DIABLO

1965

DIRECTOR: Ralph Nelson.

SCREENPLAY: Marvin H. Albert, Michel M. Grilikhes.

CAST: James Garner, Sidney Poitier, Bibi Andersson, Dennis Weaver, Bill Travers, William Redfield, John Hoyt.

Color, Not rated. 105m.

Garner is a civilian scout, bent on revenge, as he, Poitier, and Travers lead a small cavalry unit taking ammunition across hostile territory. Along the way, they're ambushed by Apaches and become involved in a battle of wits, and attrition. There's a trememdous amount of violent action in this Western, and several subplots, including Andersson as a woman on the run from her husband, Weaver. The arid Utah landscape is beautifully captured by cinematographer Charles F. Wheeler.

THE GUNFIGHTER

1950

DIRECTOR: Henry King.

SCREENPLAY: William Bowers, William Sellers.

CAST: Gregory Peck, Helen Westcott, Millard Mitchell, Jean Parker, Karl Malden, Richard Jaeckel, Skip Homeier.

B&W, Not rated, 84m.

Peck is Jimmy Ringo, an aging gunfighter whose reputation as a fast gun follows him wherever he goes. When he shows up in the small town of Cayenne to see his ex-wife (Parker) and son, the town is in upheaval, as children peer at him through the saloon window, and hothead punks get big ideas about making their own reputations by gunning him down. Peck just wants to move away with his family and start over where no one knows him, but first he has to survive. Peck is

DAVID FREEMAN

Of Human Hearts (1938). This one's interesting more in a cultural/historical way than as a satisfying drama. Jimmy Stewart is a medical student, then a Civil War surgeon. (He doesn't appear till the second half of the picture.) This is a classy venture, directed by Clarence Brown and with an MGM gloss, but it's also absurd in a particularly Hollywood way.

By the time Jimmy gets to be an army surgeon, he's too busy to write letters to his mother, who sacrificed to put him through medical school. Abraham Lincoln dresses him down for his thoughtlessness and makes him sit right down and write a letter to Mom. Abe tells him if he doesn't write regularly, he'll court-martial him.

The picture tells us more about the late-'30s America than the Civil War or anything else. People believed that although the President taking an interest in an army surgeon's correspondence habits was unusual, it wasn't impossible. FDR was the President, and didn't he care about each and every one of us? People might have found it a little pushed, a little Hollywood, but they found it moving.

The Lusty Men (1952). Robert Mitchum as a rodeo rider in the modern West. It's directed by Nicholas Ray, the least known of the great American auteurist directors. Several writers worked on the script, including Horace McCoy, though Mitchum and Ray rewrote it during production. The opening image is Mitchum in the chute, about to drop onto a Brahma bull. He's in a state of exuberance, a man in his prime. Soon enough, he's injured and has to stop all his rough riding. He's then seen in a famously stunning long shot, limping across the fairground, gear over his shoulder, wind blowing around him. He exudes self-reliance. You can feel him thinking, "I've done this to myself, now I'll live with it." With Arthur Kennedy and Susan Hayward.

A Foreign Affair (1948). Billy Wilder's comedy about post-war Berlin. With John Lund, Jean Arthur, and Marlene Dietrich. The critics of the time hated this, calling it vulgar and tasteless. It led to Wilder's reputation as a cynic. Cynical it is, and that's its glory. The picture uses footage of Berlin right after the war. Dietrich gives one of her best performances.

The Story of GI Joe (1945). Robert Mitchum in the performance that made him a star. He plays a martyred hero of the Italian campaign. Based on Ernie Pyle's war dispatches, the picture was directed by William Wellman in a documentary style that was unusual then and is unequalled now. James Agee said of it, "The closing scene seems to me a war poem as great and as beautiful as any of Whitman's."

David Freeman is a screenwriter, author of the story collection *A Hollywood Education,* and frequent contributor to *The New Yorker.* He lives in Los Angeles.

splendid as the disenchanted, world-weary gunslinger in this, the original, and the best of the gunfighter Westerns. Atmospheric b&w photography by Arthur Miller shows the town and its people in stark reality. Oscar nomination for the original story by William Bowers and Andre de Toth.

THE HANGING TREE

1959

DIRECTOR: Delmer Daves.

SCREENPLAY: Wendell Mayes, Halsted Welles.

CAST: Gary Cooper, Karl Malden, Maria Schell, Ben Piazza, George C. Scott.

Color, Not rated, 106m.

Doc Joseph Frail (Cooper) moves to a small mining camp in Montana with a six-shooter, a temper, and a past. Soon after arriving, he cares for the victim of a stagecoach holdup (Schell) who's been temporarily blinded from sun exposure after being left to die. His unacknowledged feelings for her lead to outrage when he learns that she's been raped by her business partner, Malden. Cooper is peerless as the mysterious doctor, and Malden is convincing as the miner with an ugly streak. Filmed in the beautiful Cascade Mountains by Ted McCord. Scott appears in his first film role as a loony preacher. Academy Award nomination for the title song by Jerry Livingston and Mack David, sung by Marty Robbins.

HEARTS OF THE WEST

1975

DIRECTOR: Howard Zieff.

SCREENPLAY: Rob Thompson.

CAST: Jeff Bridges, Blythe Danner, Alan Arkin, Andy Griffith, Donald Pleasence, Brad Dourif, Joseph Cotten, Geoffrey Lewis.

Color, PG rated, 102m.

It's 1929, and Lewis Tater (Bridges), an Iowa farm boy, heads out to Hollywood to pursue his dream of becoming a screenwriter for Westerns. There he meets the lovely Danner, who helps him get a job as a stunt man in B Westerns, and for a brief time, he becomes a cowboy star. This low-key spoof of Westerns and the Hollywood of the time has a wonderfully amiable atmosphere and very likable characters. Arkin is ter-

rific as the archetypical movie director, complete with riding pants, whose major obsession is not spending too much money. The ever reliable Bridges heads a first-rate cast.

JUBAL

1956

DIRECTOR: Delmer Daves.

SCREENPLAY: Russell S. Hughes, Delmer Daves, from *Jubal Troop* by Paul Wellman.

CAST: Glenn Ford, Ernest Borgnine, Rod Steiger, Valerie French, Felicia Farr, Noah Beery, Jr., Charles Bronson.

Color, Not rated, 101m.

Ford is a roaming cowboy who hires on at Borgnine's ranch, and his easygoing manner and competence soon win the approval of Borgnine, who makes him foreman. Steiger is his competition for the job, whose fury at being passed over leads to intrigue, deceit, and tragedy, involving Borgnine's restless young wife, Farr. This psychological Western, which bears more than a passing resemblance to Shakespeare's *Othello,* has a lot of talk, but there's still plenty of ropin' and ridin' amidst beautiful scenery, with strong performances by the leads.

LONELY ARE THE BRAVE

1962

DIRECTOR: David Miller.

SCREENPLAY: Dalton Trumbo, from the novel *Brave Cowboy* by Edward Abbey.

CAST: Kirk Douglas, Gena Rowlands, Walter Matthau, Michael Kane, Carroll O'Connor.

B&W, Not rated, 107m.

In this contemporary Western, Douglas is a cowboy loner who spends most of his time in the foothills, as far as possible from the traps of the modern world. When he comes down to visit old friends Kane and Rowlands, he gets entangled with the law, and is hunted down as he tries once again to escape into the mountains on horseback. Douglas is commendable as the doomed cowboy, and Matthau gives a winning performance as the laid-back local sheriff who has to track him down. This is an underrated minor classic, with good action, strong performances and a well-crafted script by Dalton Trumbo.

MCCABE AND MRS. MILLER

1971

DIRECTOR: Robert Altman.

SCREENPLAY: Robert Altman, Brian McKay, from the novel *McCabe* by Edmund Naughton.

CAST: Warren Beatty, Julie Christie, Rene Auberjonois, Hugh Millais, Keith Carradine, William Devane, Shelley Duvall.

Color, R rated, 121m.

John McCabe (Beatty) is a big-talking, small-time gambler who builds a saloon and lavish brothel in a mining town in the Northwest. He hires the delectable and equally ambitious Christie as a madam to run the place, and business is so good, the local mining company wants in, and they want Beatty out. Beatty and Christie are at their best in this unforgettable drama about greed and love. Set at the turn of the century, Altman had an entire mining town built near Vancouver, British Columbia, which adds an authentic dark and moist atmosphere to the film. Leonard Cohen contributes the songs. Christie received an Oscar nomination.

MAN OF THE WEST

1958

DIRECTOR: Anthony Mann.

SCREENPLAY: Reginald Rose, from *The Border Jumpers* by Will C. Brown.

CAST: Gary Cooper, Lee J. Cobb, Jack Lord, Julie London, Arthur O'Connell.

Color, Not rated, 100m.

This dark and brooding Western features Cooper as a man who can't shake his outlaw past. After being raised in a life of crime, Cooper tries to start anew, only to be pulled back when his villainous uncle (Cobb) threatens to kill two innocent people (O'Connell and London) if Cooper doesn't help his gang rob a bank. Cobb is chilling as the mean old man who would shoot his own mother. Jack Lord has his first big role as one of the nasty gang members. Ignored when it was released, perhaps because of its dark character, it deserves better.

THE NAKED SPUR

1953

DIRECTOR: Anthony Mann.

SCREENPLAY: Sam Rolfe, Harold Jack Bloom.

CAST: James Stewart, Janet Leigh, Ralph Meeker, Robert Ryan, Millard Mitchell.

Color, Not rated, 91m.

This stunning-looking film, shot high in the Rockies, has Stewart on the trail of bad guy Ryan. He's out for vengeance and a $5,000 reward. Along the way, he picks up a couple of hangers-on (Meeker and Mitchell) who hope they'll be able to horn in on the bounty money. There's plenty of action in this colorful, entertaining adventure. Ryan is dynamite as the sneering, sarcastic outlaw, and Stewart is fine as the harried bounty hunter. Nominated for an Academy Award for its trenchant screenplay. Beautifully photographed by William Mellor.

RIDE THE HIGH COUNTRY

1962

DIRECTOR: Sam Peckinpah.

SCREENPLAY: N. B. Stone Jr.

CAST: Joel McCrea, Randolph Scott, Edgar Buchanan, Mariette Hartley, R. G. Armstrong, James Drury, Warren Oates, Ronald Starr.

Color, Not rated, 94m.

Peckinpah puts it all together in this nearly perfect Western about two aging gunfighters who reunite to transport a gold shipment. McCrea is just looking to do a job and get paid, but Scott and his young sidekick (Starr) have bigger things in mind. McCrea and Scott give memorable, poignant performances, in a cast that's great right down to the bit players (look for Edgar Buchanan as a drunken judge). The magnificent scenery is captured by cinematographer Lucien Ballard. They don't get any better than this! This was Scott's last film.

THERE WAS A CROOKED MAN...

1970

DIRECTOR: Joseph L. Mankiewiez.

SCREENPLAY: David Newman, Robert Benton.

CAST: Kirk Douglas, Henry Fonda, Hume Cronyn, Warren Oates, Burgess Meredith, John Randolph.

Color, R rated, 123m.

Douglas is a wily outlaw with a sunny dispositon, who makes the best of it when he gets tossed into an Arizona prison. But his thriving black-market operation is in jeopardy when the straight-laced sheriff who'd arrested him (Fonda) is appointed warden. Fonda immediately initiates reforms that cramp Douglas's style, and he sets to work on an escape plan. This extravagant comedy-Western is bursting with absurdly overdrawn characters and lots of laughs.

3:10 TO YUMA

1957

DIRECTOR: Delmer Daves.

SCREENPLAY: Halsted Welles, from a story by Elmore Leonard.

CAST: Glenn Ford, Van Heflin, Felicia Farr, Leora Dana, Henry Jones, Richard Jaeckel, Robert Emhardt.

B&W, Not rated, 92m.

Financially strapped farmer Heflin accepts a job escorting murderer Ford to prison in Yuma. While waiting for the train, Heflin holes up with Ford in a hotel room, knowing that Ford's ruthless gang has taken over the town and is right outside the door. Ford is cocky, confident that Heflin will slip up as he works on his mind, trying to rattle him. This tension-filled psychological drama succeeds because of the strong performances of Ford, in an unusual departure from his good-guy roles, and Heflin as the stalwart farmer. The threat of violence is always there, just under the surface, and the suspense builds nicely to the big finale as they try to reach the waiting train.

THE TIN STAR

1957

DIRECTOR: Anthony Mann.

SCREENPLAY: Dudley Nichols, from a story by Barney Slater and Joel Kane.

CAST: Henry Fonda, Anthony Perkins, Betsy Palmer, Neville Brand, John McIntire.

B&W, Not rated, 93m.

Inexperienced young sheriff Perkins is besieged by problems when bounty hunter Fonda shows up in town to collect his fee. Fonda, a former sheriff, takes pity on the kid and shows him the basics of the fast draw and staying alive. Perkins has to deal with menacing tough guy Brand in a showdown.

Good performances all around with Fonda cool, calm and unruffled, and Perkins scared, but determined to do the job. McIntire is good as the crusty, sardonic doctor. A very satisfying, well-made Western. The story and screenplay were nominated for Oscars. Trick-shot artist Rodd Redwing makes an appearance. Score by Elmer Bernstein.

WINCHESTER 73

1950

DIRECTOR: Anthony Mann.

SCREENPLAY: Robert L. Richards, Borden Chase, from a story by Stuart N. Lake.

CAST: James Stewart, Shelley Winters, Dan Duryea, Stephen McNally, John McIntire, Millard Mitchell.

B&W, Not rated, 92m.

Stewart is looking for his father's murderer and the Winchester 73 rifle that he won in a July 4th contest. The gun was stolen after the contest by the loser, McNally, who proceeded to lose it in a card game. From there it passes from owner to owner, as Stewart tracks it down. Stewart is great here, and there's a lot of wisecracking humor. Rock Hudson appears as one of the string of owners of the gun, an Indian warrior, complete with face paint! A young Tony Curtis is in the cavalry. This great entertainment has been credited with the resurgence of the Western in the 1950s.

Index

The index has been arranged along three broad categorical lines: film title, director, and principal actor(s). Film titles appear in italics. Directors' names are followed by the abbreviation (dir.); all other names are those of actors.

C

H

I

J

K

O

P

Q

R

T

Y

Z

If you enjoyed this book and want to share with the authors you suggestions for movies that many might have missed, please feel free to contact them at the following address:

Ardis Sillick and Michael McCormick
Toledo, IA 52342-9413

CCSMJC@well.com